COTSWOLD
STONE HOMES

HISTORY · CONSERVATION · CARE

COTSWOLD STONE HOMES

HISTORY · CONSERVATION · CARE

MICHAEL HILL AND SALLY BIRCH
PHOTOGRAPHS BY MARGARET LISTER

Foreword by John Julius Norwich

SUTTON PUBLISHING

First published in the United Kingdom in 1994 by
Alan Sutton Publishing Ltd, an imprint of Sutton Publishing Limited,
Phoenix Mill · Thrupp · Stroud · Gloucestershire GL5 2BU

This paperback edition first published in 1998 by Sutton Publishing Limited

British Library Cataloguing in Publication Data

A catalogue record for this book is available from the British Library.

ISBN 0-7509-1796-2

Frontispiece: A house in Nailsworth showing the tall gables and window details
which are typical of Cotswold stone architecture.

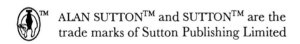 ALAN SUTTON™ and SUTTON™ are the
trade marks of Sutton Publishing Limited

Typeset in 11/14 Baskerville MT.
Typesetting and origination by
Sutton Publishing Limited.
Printed in Great Britain by
WBC Limited, Bridgend, Mid-Glamorgan.

CONTENTS

FOREWORD

Of all the building materials known to man, stone is the noblest and the most durable; and of all the building stones of England, Cotswold is the loveliest. It carries with it none of the potential pomposity of Portland, or the inevitable austerity of granite. It is, essentially, a country stone: a stone for villages rather than cities, for manor houses rather than palaces; a stone, rich and mellow as honey, that seems to have soaked up centuries of sunshine – which, with its own gentle radiance, it now returns.

It is also a stone of inspiration. Partly because of its intrinsic beauty, partly owing to its softness and ease of working during those first months out of the quarry, it has from the first encouraged the Cotswold masons to develop a style of their own, as perfectly suited to the stone itself as to the surrounding countryside. Of this style the dominant feature proves, again and again, to be the gable. Cotswold gables rise as high as the roof-ridges; they are adorned, as likely as not, with elaborate finials; they enclose within them mullioned windows surmounted by beautifully moulded dripstones, while those in the centre may also boast incised labels with the initials of the builder and, perhaps, a date. But the gables are not all. Every feature of the building, whether it be manor or cottage, shares the same meticulousness, the same attention to form, proportion and detail; and all is held together, and is given its character and strength, by the warm magic of the stone.

This book is a celebration of Cotswold building; but it is also a warning. Like almost everything beautiful in England, the Cotswold tradition is under threat – from modern materials, modern building techniques, modern money. It can be preserved only by knowledge and understanding: two vital necessities which the authors – Trustees of the Woodchester Mansion Trust, which promotes training in local stonemasonry and conservation – possess in full measure. The pages that follow should be required reading not only for all those fortunate enough to live in a Cotswold house, but for everyone, everywhere, who cares about English architecture. Mark them well.

JOHN JULIUS NORWICH

ACKNOWLEDGEMENTS

The authors would like to thank the following people and organizations for their generous assistance: Janet Barber, Captain John Barrow of Farmington Quarry, David Brill, John Byrne, Peter Causon, Tom Chester, Cotswold District Council, Sir Anthony Denny, Charles Dickins, Ashley Dickinson, Alison Durham, Sheila Ely, Judith and John Exelby, Toby and Ursula Falconer, Mary Fell, Mr J. Foster, Gloucestershire County Council, Gloucestershire Wildlife Trust, John Goom, Cecil Haslam, Clifford Hooper, Mr and Mrs James Marshall, Barry Mason, Robert and Muriel Parsons, David and Gill Playne, David Pollard of The Underground Quarry at Corsham, Arthur Price, Mrs Pat Quinn, Canon Hedley Ringrose, John Snellgrove, Michael Speed, Barry Stow, Michael Thorndyke, Julian Usborne, Roy Vallis of Stroud District Council, Jamie Vans, David and Linda Viner, Lionel Walrond, the Woodchester Mansion Trust and the Friends of the Mansion, and Rory Young.

All the photographs in this book were taken by Margaret Lister and the authors, except for the photographs and illustrations provided, with permission for reproduction, by the following: David Brill for the use of the map of the Cotswolds, the Cotswold Countryside Collection at Northleach, Toby Falconer, Peckhams of Stroud, David Pollard, and the Royal Commission on the Historical Monuments of England.

Editorial Note

This book is intended to be a descriptive guide to the subject of Cotswold stone and its uses, and NOT an instruction manual. Neither the authors, the publisher, nor any person or organization mentioned or connected with the subject in any way, can take any responsibility for accidents or damage arising from application of the information, materials or procedures described in the book. Readers are advised to consult the appropriate professionals, craftsmen and specialists before taking any action. The views expressed are the authors' own and do not necessarily reflect those of either Cotswold District Council or the Woodchester Mansion Trust.

PREFACE

Throughout – and far beyond – the many landscapes of the British Isles, the Cotswolds are justly renowned for their beauty. But what is it that constitutes their particular attraction? The windswept wolds are pleasantly spacious, but they are not as romantically wild as Dartmoor or Yorkshire. The valleys are charming, but not as cosy as those of Devon or as dramatic as those of Wales. The typical architecture is modest, almost severe: no ornate timberwork, no colourful bricks; no dramas, no extremes. There is an atmosphere of polite privacy, and a timelessness which holds ancient mysteries in reserve. These qualities make the Cotswold landscape quintessentially English. Indeed, the typical picture-postcard view of a Cotswold cottage has become a cliché, a symbol for 'Old England' which is recognized around the world.

The single element which unites the Cotswolds is the local limestone. Nowhere else in Britain is stone so mild and mellow, and its use so sympathetic with its surroundings. The traditional cottages appear simply to have grown up out of the ground; and as they grow old, they seem to melt gently back into it. It is all so settled that it is taken as natural, and yet it is not so at all. The Cotswold landscape is very much a man-made one. Because the overall character of it was made by men of past centuries – in some cases long past – there is sometimes a sense that it should not, or even cannot, be changed. But not to change is to die; and the challenge is not to evade change, but to direct it in ways that maintain the essential identity of the region without damaging or fossilizing it.

To a certain extent this is the responsibility of every Cotswold inhabitant and visitor, but it is perhaps most important for those who are involved with the fundamental factor – stone. People who live in Cotswold stone, work with it, construct or demolish it, own, use, buy or sell it, are playing a part in the continuing creation of the Cotswolds. This book aims to provide a better understanding of Cotswold stone to help us handle this responsibility to our own satisfaction, and to the benefit of both present and future generations.

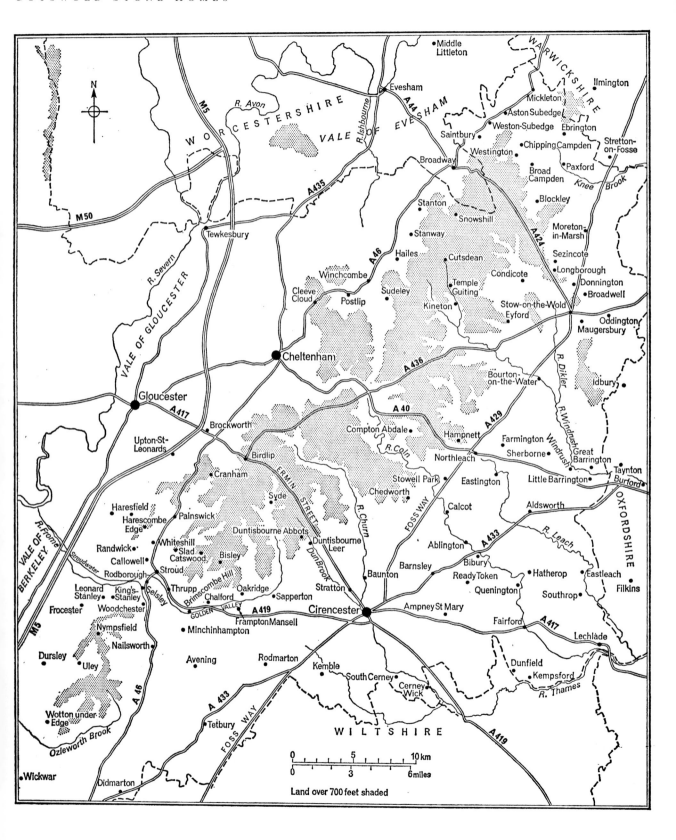

Land over 700 feet shaded

Chapter 1

LIVING IN A STONE LANDSCAPE

Cotswold stone homes and their inhabitants today are part of a pattern in time and place. The landscape, its flora and fauna, its people and their traditions, have developed alongside and influenced each other since prehistory; and the relationship is still intimate and active. Before considering Cotswold stone more closely in the next chapter, an outline of the landscape and the history of Cotswold life – animal and human, past and present – will show how such homes came into being.

Exactly what are the Cotswolds? Although the answer is often taken for granted, it is not easy to define in detail. Even the name is controversial. Some say that it derives from 'Cod's wald' or the high land belonging to Cod, a Saxon chief. Others attribute the origin to 'cotes wold' or the hills where the sheep pens or 'cotes' are found. The spelling developed from the medieval 'Coteswaud' or 'Cottyswolde' through 'Cotssold' and Shakespeare's 'Cotsall', to the version accepted today.

According to various definitions of their boundaries, the Cotswolds lie mostly in Gloucestershire, but also contain parts of Warwickshire, Oxfordshire, Avon, and Wiltshire. The region may thus be considered to be anything from 60 to 100 miles (96 to160 km) in length, and about half as wide, forming a rough lozenge shape on a north-east–south-west axis.

For many people, it is the range of hills which constitute 'The Cotswolds', from about the 500 ft (150 m) contour upwards to the highest point at Cleeve Hill near Cheltenham, 1,083 ft (330 m). Most of the high land lies between Stinchcombe in the south and Chipping Campden in the north, as indicated in the accompanying map. To the west, the escarpment – where limestone meets clay – is clearly visible; but to the east the shallow contours do not provide such a distinct boundary.

One might say that the use of Cotswold stone in buildings defines the Cotswold boundaries. Stone was, however, transported for some distance from its native quarries in the limestone strata, so there is not always a clear

Opposite
The Cotswolds have no 'official' boundary, but follow the general alignment of the Jurassic limestone belt across south-western England. (By courtesy of David Brill.)

Village springs, such as this one at Nailsworth, are now largely decorative, but were formerly the vital water supply for villagers and their livestock. Many Cotswold villages were built on the 'spring line' where limestone beds lie next to clay.

demarcation. The stone layers continue beyond the hills, from Dorset to Lincolnshire, but these regions are not considered to be part of the Cotswolds merely by virtue of their stone.

So it is not only the hills, or the limestone buildings, or even the two together which provide that elusive definition. The third necessary element is the traditional building style. As will be described later, typical Cotswold architecture was heavily influenced by the dominant sheep-rearing and wool-weaving industries based on the hills and valleys. Thus the three elements of hills, limestone building, and architecture are linked to create the region known as the Cotswolds.

The Cotswold hills are not a huge or dominant land mass. The formation is often compared to a narrow slice cut from a whole cheese, and laid on its side; the rind, as it were, forming the edge or escarpment to the west and south, while to the east the contours diminish gradually. The rivers Windrush, Leach, Coln and Churn flow eastward, towards Oxford and the headwaters of the Thames near Kemble. On the western side the waters drain towards the Severn Vale. Each side of the watershed has a distinctive character, as Herbert Evans wrote in *Highways and Byways in Oxford and the Cotswolds* (1905):

the eastern valleys are depressions in the open down, the western, deep wooded ravines. By a curious coincidence this distinction exactly corresponds to that between the water areas of the Thames and of the Severn, so that either area is in a way in harmony with the general character of its own river . . . A glance at the map will show that in the western corner the streams descend from similar altitudes in a much shorter distance, and this will go far to explain the difference in question.

Where there is limestone, there is water. All around the Cotswolds, innumerable streams thread their way intimately through villages and across ancient trackways. Such tumbling streams cut and mould the landscape at a rate that may be measured within decades rather than centuries. The Cotswold watercourses are punctuated by the sites of mills which were used to turn water into power for over a thousand years. Since limestone is so permeable, the action of water is fundamental to the formation and continuing development of the Cotswold landscape. Indeed, in many places the soil provides only the thinnest of interfaces between rock and rain, and is all too easily swept away by heavy rain and floods. Sudden changes in underground water levels give rise to new springs, sometimes powerful enough to lift the tarmac off roads.

The Cotswolds were crossed by roads before most other parts of Britain. Roman roads, straight and confident, radiate like the spokes of a wheel from

Wells and pumps were used to bring water to the surface where there was no convenient spring. An old pump at Little Barrington fed water into a stone trough, and no doubt also acted as a focus for the social life of the village.

Cirencester. The Foss Way runs from north-east to south-west and provides a 'spine' road for the region. Nowadays its course is followed by the A429, running from Lincoln to Bath through such typically Cotswold towns as Moreton-in-Marsh, Stow-on-the-Wold and Northleach. Also out of Cirencester, the A417 follows the Ermin Way, and the B4425 takes the old Akeman Street.

Ever-increasing motor traffic has profound implications for the local environment and its stone buildings. Many of the roads and village streets were designed for pack-horses rather than cars – let alone lorries and buses – and the dirt and corrosion caused by exhaust fumes have an all-too-visible effect on the stone buildings which lie beside busy roads. It is a tragic irony that buildings which have withstood everything the natural elements could hurl at them over hundreds of years, are now becoming maimed and rotten within a very few decades.

There is no large urban centre-point of the Cotswolds, a factor which must have contributed to the preservation of its traditional charm; the region might

Where the Foss Way runs through the broad centre of Moreton-in-Marsh it has always provided an excellent site for a market. The inevitable bustle and congestion was once caused by farm carts and livestock, but now consists of cars, buses and lorries.

Opposite
A bird's-eye view from the church tower in Cirencester encompasses many centuries of Cotswold living, from the distant avenues of Cirencester Park and its stately house (1714), to the museum of Roman remains, medieval cottages, and modern shops of the town.

otherwise have become little more than a green belt around a modern city. But the nearest cities – Bristol, Gloucester, Oxford, Bath, and the large town of Cheltenham – lie beyond the Cotswold fringes. Within the hills themselves, one of the most densely populated areas is around Stroud, where small ancient villages and modern developments have merged together in a lively, if unattractive, muddle. Cirencester, once the Roman city of Corinium – then the second most important city of Britain – is the largest and most central Cotswold town, and provides modern amenities while maintaining the Cotswold character. Cheltenham, despite its proximity to the scarp, has little vernacular Cotswold atmosphere, being more akin to Bath in its Georgian gentility. Industrial and cosmopolitan Gloucester is historically less concerned with the Cotswolds than with the Severn and a world of trade.

While these cities and towns undoubtedly influence Cotswold life, this is essentially a region of villages. Many, such as Bibury or Bourton-on-the-Water, have become famous simply for being old and pretty. While the houses have not changed in centuries, the communities are now likely to be very different in structure. Cotswold village society now often comprises all sorts of people, relatively few of them born and bred in the region, and even fewer following traditional local occupations.

The Natural Life of the Cotswolds

Before human beings came to the region, or even existed, there were animals. The vast treasury of fossils embedded in Cotswold stone includes the remains of some of Britain's largest dinosaurs. Much of the fossil skeleton of a plesiosaur was uncovered at Blockley in 1990. It would have lived about 190 million years ago. These swan-necked, paddle-footed swimming dinosaurs were typical of the fauna of shallow prehistoric seas. Numerous fossilized bones of a cetiosaurus were found in 1988 at Hornsleasow Quarry, near Moreton-in-Marsh, within a shallow layer of clay between two limestone layers, indicating that the landscape of the time consisted of low-lying wooded plains with lakes and pools. The cetiosaurus would have been about 60 ft (18 m) long, resembling the well-known apatosaurus (formerly called brontosaurus).

More recent finds of large fossils date to the end of the last Ice Age, about 10,000 years ago. A tusk of a woolly mammoth was found at Cainscross, near Stroud, in 1892, and mammoths' teeth are quite commonly found just east of the Cotswolds, in gravel pits. Other large mammals of that period, which would have been hunted by the earliest inhabitants, included the woolly rhinoceros; the giant deer with its 12 ft (3.6 m) span of antlers; large red deer;

The sweeping horns of an old English longhorn cow discourage approach to her calf. The breed, once the most common in England, may trace descent from the great prehistoric aurochs or wild cattle which roamed the ancient woodland of the region.

and the huge, heavy-horned wild cattle, or aurochs, which may even have survived until the coming of the Romans. The splitting-away of Britain from the rest of the European land mass, which occurred only 7,500 years ago, contributed to the extinction of large prehistoric species.

Some of the Cotswold mammals which would have been familiar to the earliest human tribes are still in evidence today. Hares (fondly claimed, by the old Cotswold shepherds, to be 'as big as donkeys') may be seen on the stony fields of the high wolds. Foxes are common all over the Cotswolds, adapting happily to town and village life, undeterred by the occasional forays of red-coated huntsmen and baying hounds. Badgers survive in good numbers, especially in the secret wooded valleys, and most other British mammals are found in the Cotswolds. Some mammals, such as fallow deer and grey squirrels, have been introduced.

The wildlife of the region is typical of many other parts of southern Britain, and is associated naturally with the kind of light deciduous woodland which once covered the area. Little of this 'ancient' woodland – as at Chedworth, Guiting, and Oakley Woods – now remains, and the fauna which survives has done so by adapting to a man-made landscape. While he has mainly destroyed wildlife habitats, man has, however, created certain ecological 'niches' from the native stone. These include dry-stone walls; stone quarries

A rooftop nature reserve: as decades pass, a stone-slated roof gradually accumulates moss, lichens, climbing plants and even rooted wild flowers. These, in turn, provide food and shelter for insects, small mammals and birds.

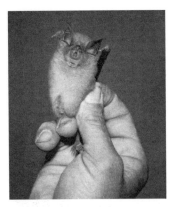

A Greater Horseshoe Bat comes under scientific scrutiny. This rare species roosts in several old underground quarries in the region. Other bats, all protected by law, may inhabit stone barns and the attics of Cotswold homes.

(including the underground ones commonly called 'mines'); and, obviously, stone buildings.

It is part of the picturesque charm of old stone-roofed houses that they carry quite a variety of lichens, mosses, ivy, even wild flowers and shrubs on their roofs. Larger stone buildings such as barns always contained rats and mice, and barn owls nesting in the timbers. It is the spread of intensive agriculture, not just the adaptation of barns to modern dwellings, which has contributed to the current 'critical' status of the barn owl in the Cotswolds. They need suitable hunting territory – rough grassland and wood edges – close to their nesting site. Their population in Gloucestershire had decreased by nearly 70 per cent to 35 breeding pairs at the last count, nearly a decade ago. The sight of this large bird, flying silently through the dusk, is now an extremely rare treat.

While it might not be thought that much could live in the cold, darkness and damp of an old underground stone quarry, this is an agreeable environment for several species of bat. Plenty of hanging space, peace, and constant temperature and humidity, are just what they need for successful hibernation and roosting. For this reason, underground quarries in the Cotswolds are among the last refuges of some rare British bats, including the Greater and Lesser Horseshoe species. Bats will also roost in large airy house attics; they are protected by law, and they do no harm, so their presence should be considered a privilege.

Another man-made stone environment which has proved important for wildlife is the traditional Cotswold dry-stone wall. It is the wildlife equivalent of a large town, providing food, hiding and living space for a wide variety of creatures, and may also act as a wildlife corridor, linking habitats such as woods and ponds. Insects and spiders abound in the myriad crevices, alongside worms, slugs and snails. Underneath fallen or discarded stones, toads, slow-worms, and the occasional grass snake may be found. Shrews, mice and voles are hunted by weasels and stoats. Hedgehogs hibernate among the piles of leaves and dead grass at the foot of a wall. Small birds seek out food, and may also nest in safe niches covered by vegetation. Songbirds use the topping stones to sing their territory; thrushes use them as snail-smashing anvils; grey squirrels, as pathways. It is an extraordinarily rich and busy world of wildlife, which should in itself be reason enough to preserve existing dry-stone walls, and to build more.

Most stone walls are old, but it is often hard to know just how old. Since there is a rough rule of thumb to estimate the age of a hedge – roughly one species per century – it would be useful to know a similar way of dating stonework: nature may yet provide an answer. There is currently some research being carried out to determine whether the size of lichens is

Left
A cloud of cow-parsley almost submerges a crumbling dry-stone wall in the north Cotswolds. These characteristic walls are disappearing from the landscape at an alarming rate – with severe environmental, as well as aesthetic, consequences.

Right
The size of lichens and the dates on tombstones may combine to provide clues as to the dating of historic stonework elsewhere in the Cotswolds.

consistent with the age of the buildings on which they grow. In particular, the growth rate of lichens on gravestones is being studied, as the stonework can, of course, be dated accurately from the inscription. Unfortunately, however, lichens grow slowly – perhaps only half a millimetre in diameter a year – and not at a consistent rate; and there are obviously other factors which may influence lichen growth, such as climatic changes, or simply cleaning of the stone. Where the age of a building or dry-stone wall is known, however, a study of the relative sizes of the different lichens would always be interesting and possibly scientifically useful.

Human Habitation in the Cotswolds

Most of the stone walls which remain were built within the last couple of centuries, but humans started to affect the natural history of the Cotswolds very much earlier. About 5000 BC the region consisted mainly of woodland in which oak, elm, lime and hazel trees predominated, some of which were felled by the mesolithic tribes. Less than two thousand years later, neolithic tribesmen from the continent, using stone axes, started to clear the forest in earnest to make settlements, building houses, defences, and animal stockades with the timber. They used the woodlands for many purposes – building timber and firewood, tools, foodstuffs, charcoal burning and others – but grazing became more important. The tree cover was gradually pushed back until much of the Cotswold area had been turned into grassy downs and patches of arable land.

While timber was the most readily available and easily worked building material, the local stone – particularly the Great Oolite – was used for monoliths and communal graves. Some of these tumuli (or, in Gloucestershire dialect, 'tumps') demonstrate considerable skill in dry-stone walling, and it has been suggested that there were 'professional' tomb builders of the time. There are hundreds of such sites in various states of repair in the Cotswolds, notably at Belas Knap near Cheltenham and Hetty Pegler's Tump near Uley.

About 1800 BC the Neolithic Age gave way to the Bronze Age, whose peoples adapted a knowledge of metal working brought from their mainland European background to make household implements, tools, armour and ornaments. Their graves were smaller, round, usually individual, but their stone circles and monoliths were often of striking size. The largest remaining stone circle in the Cotswold area is the Rollright Stones, straddling the Oxfordshire/Warwickshire border: evocatively named the King's Stone, the King's Men, and the Whispering Knights, these are the subject of legends.

The Bronze Age was in turn supplanted, about a thousand years later, by the Iron Age: Celtic tribes built large fortified 'camps', traded iron bars, cremated their dead, and lived in longhouses with their livestock. They developed a rich culture incorporating cereal crops, ploughs, carts, coinage, pottery and jewellery. Among the most important were the Dobunni, a Belgic tribe whose settlement at Bagendon enclosed 200 acres (80 ha) within fortified ditches. Since there is no evidence of a battle here, it was possibly due to the collaborative policy of these Dobunni that the invading Romans, after AD 43, decided to construct their major city of Corinium (Cirencester) nearby.

The Romans accelerated the conversion of ancient woodland to sheep grazing downs, and developed a very important wool trade with mainland Europe. The affluence of the region can be inferred from the remains of large Roman settlements such as those at Cirencester, Whitcombe, and Chedworth. At Woodchester the enormous and elegant Roman mosaic pavement, nowadays left buried underground for safe keeping, indicates a country palace fit for the regional governor. Apart from developing trade and building roads, there is some evidence that the Romans brought Christianity to the

The King's Men, forming a circle about 100 ft (30 m) in diameter, are part of the group called the Rollright Stones and, according to legend, are a would-be King of England with his Knights and Men, who were petrified by a witch.

Cotswolds. There is even a local tradition that St Paul came here in the course of his travels.

After the Romans departed, around AD 400, there was a decline in Cotswold prosperity until the Saxons invaded, winning Bath, Gloucester and Cirencester in 577. Fifty years later they in turn were confronted by warriors from Mercia, who took the major part of the northern Cotswolds under the banner of the Northumbrian princes. This area became known as the territory of the Hwicce and the Northumbrian influence included the spread of Christianity, while the Saxons, to the south, remained largely heathen for some time. By the ninth and tenth centuries, however, the Church was becoming established, and building in stone; several churches which survive to this day (such as those at Winstone and Daglingworth) have Saxon parts, now a millennium old.

The Normans, after their occupation in 1066, continued the use of Cotswold stone in churches, and also in those symbols of a dominant culture – castles. None of the latter survives intact in the region, having been destroyed, or incorporated into later buildings, as at Beverston. The established affluence of the Cotswolds was indicated in Domesday Book, that remarkable national survey initiated by William the Conqueror at the Christmas Court in Gloucester in 1085. The pattern of sheep grazing and

Last revealed to archaeologists and the public in 1973, the Roman mosaic pavement at Woodchester has since been left interred to preserve it from damage. One of the largest – about 50 ft (15 m) square – and finest of such mosaics, the main section depicts the Roman deity Orpheus with a variety of animals.

corn growing lasted for the following six or seven centuries, after which stone quarrying became a third major Cotswold industry. Gradually the particular beauty of Cotswold stone began to be prized beyond these hills, and transported – with great difficulty and cost – to distant cities, for grand and glorious buildings such as St Paul's Cathedral and the Palace of Westminster. Such difficulty and cost precluded its use for common or vernacular buildings.

It was during the Middle Ages that the Cotswold landscape took on the shape which – apart from the widespread later use of stone in walls and vernacular buildings – it essentially retains today. Some land was privately owned, freehold; much was owned by lords of manors, or by the bishops and abbots of the great churches, and rented out to farmers and shepherds; some was common land, exploited according to the numbers, needs and status of the local population. The land was almost everyone's living, and therefore

In a timeless scene, money and horses change hands on Charter Day at Stow-on-the-Wold. Each year, thousands of Romany gypsies from all over Britain meet to socialize, trade, and keep their ancient traditions very much alive.

jealously guarded according to an accretion of laws, customs and understandings. Contemporary accounts of court cases arising from conflict over land use show that the serene contours of the Cotswolds disguised a legal minefield. Conflict sometimes continued for generations, and not infrequently led to physical confrontation.

The fertile fields of the Middle Ages were ploughed in the manner known as 'ridge and furrow', the single plough-board throwing up earth to one side only and thus gradually building up a series of parallel ridges. These usually ran with the slope of the land rather than with the contour, thus improving what was already good drainage. The striped pattern of such land can still be seen in many parts of the Cotswolds, being most evident in low light or under a dusting of snow.

In conjunction with maps, field names, and large boundary marker stones, these ridges could be numbered, to help demarcate one man's land from his neighbour's. Blocks of ploughed land were also called 'furlongs', and were added to along their edges by the clearance of small parcels of land called 'assarts'. This constant process of nibbling at ancient woodland resulted in the major part of the Cotswolds having been cleared for farming and sheep-runs by the thirteenth century.

An abundance of food and income bred larger, healthier families and attracted settlers from outside. The resulting pressure of population increase

A Cotswold ewe suckles her twin lambs at Naunton. This breed, now rare, was in former times indirectly responsible for shaping the Cotswold landscape, and giving rise to a prosperous international trade.

halved the average family land holdings within two hundred years of Domesday Book. The outbreak of plague in 1348 – the Black Death – wiped out many communities and villages, but it was not the only factor in the down-swing of the Cotswold population of that period. The expansion of sheep-farming, with lords of the manor keeping many thousands of sheep and turning much arable land into grazing pasture, may have contributed to the death of small communities. The peasant farmer simply could not compete, and in many areas over-grazing was a serious problem.

It is a pity that the Cotswold breed of sheep, upon whose broad back this empire was founded, is now rare and little-known. Few exist today, and it is believed that only one large flock of Cotswold sheep still grazes its native wolds, near Naunton. But once 'the Cotswold lion', as the breed was called, was famous for its large, sturdy build, and the thick wool falling into a 'lovelock' over its arched face. A single fleece – long, dense and curly, and coloured creamy-buff like the local stone – might weigh 14 lb (6.35 kg). Indeed, the old English weight equivalent of 14 lb = 1 stone was based on a standardized block of stone hoisted inside a barn to weigh fleeces. Half a stone in weight (7 lb, or 3.2 kg) was known as a 'clove'; 2 stones constituted a 'tod'. In 1480 the wool merchant William Midwinter complained that 'wool in Cotswold is at a great price, 13s. 4d. a tod'; by the following year it had exceeded 14s. a tod. There were 13 tods to a sack, and 2.5 sacks to a 'sarpler' – a huge bale wrapped in canvas for transport to London and the continent. It was a major industry even by today's standards, and so important for the whole country that the Lord Chancellor in Parliament took the 'Woolsack' of Cotswold wool as his traditional seat.

Cotswold wool, and later woven cloth, was exported around the world from the ports of Gloucester, Bristol, Southampton and London, a trade which has only declined within the past century. The social hierarchy of the wool industry – from the landowners to the farmers, shepherds and shearers, weavers, mill-managers and workers, fullers, dyers, and many others – shaped the built environment of the Cotswolds. Almost all of them were housed in stone by the end of the eighteenth century. With the great forests gone, building timber was now in short supply and quarries were opened up everywhere to provide building material. Grand mansions were built in manicured parks; towns, with their shopkeepers and professional classes, developed from village markets. Meanwhile the wool workers were housed in tiny cottages, often crammed together higgledy-piggledy, as at Chalford, on steep hillsides which were unsuitable for sheep-runs but close to the valley mills.

After woodland clearance and stone building, it took one further change to transform the rural Cotswolds of ancient times into what is essentially the landscape of today: enclosure. This began in the sixteenth century and gathered pace to peak in the eighteenth and early nineteenth centuries. A series of Parliamentary Acts administered by local commissioners enclosed more than a quarter of the Cotswold landscape. In some places, hedges were planted; but rubble stones were easily available, and walls could be quickly built when labour was cheap.

Thus the familiar dry-stone walls were built all over the Cotswolds. Walls enclosed the remaining light woodland to make hunting parks for the aristocracy. Walls partitioned the strips of arable land. Most importantly, walls segmented the great open sweeps of common grazing land. When one stands today on one of the few remnants of open common, such as Minchinhampton Common or Cleeve Hill, it is not the same as it must have been in pre-enclosure days – buildings, roads, golf courses and telegraph poles set a modern mark on the landscape – but one can begin to imagine the airy, open, rolling hills of ancient Cotswold. Of some 5,000 acres (2,000 ha) of commons remaining in Gloucestershire, 71 per cent are in the Cotswolds.

Some tenants managed to establish claim to areas of land, others were recompensed with allotments, but inevitably many peasants were elbowed out. The sheer extent of walling necessary for some properties was a heavy expense for the farmers. The appearance of the region was further changed

During the eighteenth and nineteenth centuries many large and self-contained farmsteads were built in the Cotswolds. Some have now become derelict, or been converted to new uses. Others, such as this farm at Newington Bagpath, adapt to changing conditions with a busy mixture of crops and livestock.

by the necessity for farming families to build farmsteads within their own patch of land, rather than living in the nearby village; many isolated Cotswold farms thus date from around 1800, the height of the enclosure movement.

The eighteenth and early nineteenth centuries were also a time when the Cotswolds became much more 'gentrified' – the more affluent classes built mansions and fine country houses, set in gracious parks and formal gardens; and having done so, they set about visiting one another, and congregating at fashionable places such as the spas of Cheltenham and Bath.

The gentrification of the region was founded on a new affluence arising from the Industrial Revolution. The huge expansion of industry in the century from about 1750 particularly affected the south Cotswolds, where many more mills, railways and canals were built in connection with the

Winter mist adds to the forlorn appearance of St Mary's Mill at Chalford, and the overgrown canal alongside it. Formerly producing paper, cloth, and walking sticks, this mill has found a new role as a marketing and computer centre.

process of turning wool into cloth and exporting it all over the world. Stroud was transformed from a mere hamlet into a prosperous industrial town, famous for the scarlet cloth which dressed the British Army, and also for its blues. In 1826 the Revd Witts, on one of his excursions around Chalford and Woodchester, noted in his *Diary of a Cotswold Parson* that 'Machinery and millworks bestride the once limpid brooks long dyed a deep blue by the processes carried on.'

There was only so much power to be harnessed from the local water, and as demand increased coal was imported from the West Midlands. This traffic gave rise to the Stroudwater Canal (built 1775–9) linking the Severn with Stroud and the Thames & Severn Canal. In the nineteenth century, railway freight eventually overtook the canal system, although for a long time they operated (in some places, literally) side by side. The canals were finally abandoned between the 1930s and '50s and are now the subject of some noble attempts at restoration. It is only a few decades since the large canal basin at Brimscombe was drained and a range of unlovely small factories built in its place; but already it seems fantastic to imagine that barges and even multi-masted ships passed this way, between some of the steepest Cotswold hills, miles from the sea.

Although the Cotswolds were relatively unscathed by the two world wars, the departure of many men to fight – never to return, or to return to a changed social structure – contributed to the decline of traditional Cotswold agriculture. Hundreds of acres of grassland each year were subsequently turned to arable use, and machinery replaced manpower, driving more families from the farming life – as has happened throughout the country. Cereal crops including oats, wheat and barley have increased: the light, well-drained Cotswold soil suits barley particularly well. Nowadays, however, the choice of crop is dictated less by the nature of the land than by the quotas, standards and subsidies of the Common Market. Consequently the Cotswolds in summer are painted in colours they never saw before, such as the bright yellows of rape and sunflowers or the blue of linseed; and farming patterns no longer relate to the local community, but to world commodity markets.

The proliferation of building in the nineteenth and early twentieth centuries played a large part in the making of the Cotswolds landscape which we see now. Luckily the Arts and Crafts Movement, inspired by William Morris and focused largely on the Cotswolds, helped considerably to raise public awareness of the value of traditional styles and methods, and thus to preserve buildings which would otherwise have been crushed by the relentless march of development and economy. However, there was almost no control over building until the Town and Country Planning Act of 1947.

The main purpose of the Act was to stop development in open country, not for any aesthetic reasons, but to preserve agricultural land. As a result, new homes were more or less restricted to existing settlements, with large developments springing up on the fringes of Cotswold towns such as Stow-on-the-Wold and Northleach. From 1947 onwards, almost all building required planning permission. Buildings were listed if they were of particular architectural or historical merit, initially simply to prevent wholesale demolition; later refinements covered alterations to historic buildings.

The Cotswolds, like the rest of the English countryside, were further protected by Duncan Sandys' Civic Amenities Act of 1967 which introduced the concept of 'conservation areas'. Within their boundaries greater planning control is exercised to 'preserve or enhance the character or appearance of the area'. The heightened public awareness of conservation in general, together with a few decisive local campaigns, brought an increase in the number of Conservation Officers in the late 1980s. In 1992 Cotswold District

Council had more listed buildings (more than 6,000) and conservation areas (144) than any other local authority.

The increasing desirability and market value of Cotswold cottages, and the cost of repairs, has tended to force natives and long-term residents of the region out of their pretty little cottages and into housing estates. It led to the 'cottage boom' of the 1970s and '80s, when derelict hovels and crumbling barns were renovated, to varying standards, by enthusiastic new owners, quick-profit entrepreneurs, and DIY amateurs. Much current work on historic houses is concerned less with preserving the original building than with undoing (if possible) very recent mistakes.

There are two major influences on the current development of landscape and habitation patterns in the Cotswolds which have become really significant only in the past decade or two, and which are intertwined: tourism

Tourists on the bridge at Bibury reflect on the very public family life of a moorhen at her nest (near left). Visitors contribute enormously to the local community, but entail many unresolved problems.

and leisure. There is still a process of adjustment going on in local government and within communities as they seek to fit these new factors into the overall framework of Cotswold life.

The jobs of 26,000 people – one in ten of the region's workforce – are sustained by the tourist industry, worth some £200 million a year, so the implications of tourism deserve greater prominence in local environmental planning. One cannot expect tourists to contribute to the upkeep of the Cotswolds' beautiful landscape and historic buildings if they are inadequately catered for. Inept tourist management also leads to environmental pressure, and to damage which may ultimately destroy the very beauty which brings people here.

The provision of leisure facilities, for both tourists and residents, also increases pressure on the environment. This potential conflict is a concern of those responsible for the statutory Cotswolds Area of Outstanding Natural Beauty (AONB). Its specific tasks include maintaining tracks and footpaths; information and publicity; visitor accommodation; reducing environmental damage, and improving countryside management. This body also monitors the increasing number of applications for golf courses to add to the thirty-odd which already exist in and around the Cotswold area.

These and many other factors shape the society and landscape of the Cotswolds today, and provide a cultural foundation for living in a Cotswold house. The next aspect to be considered is the fabric of which such a house is made.

At Minchinhampton Common – one of the few remaining areas of common land in the Cotswolds – the traditional grazing cattle and horses must now compete for space not only with golfers, but with sightseers, dog-walkers, cyclists, and kite-flyers.

Chapter 2

COTSWOLD STONE

The rocks from which Cotswold building stone is extracted are among the youngest in the British Isles, although 'young' seems a strange term to apply to material created nearly 200 million years ago. Considering their relatively small area of the earth's surface, the British Isles comprise rocks from a remarkably wide variety of geological periods and formations. Broadly speaking, the rocks are oldest in the north-west and youngest in the south-east, ranging from the volcanic gneiss of north-west Scotland and the Outer Hebridean Islands, at 3,000 million years old, to the clays and sands of up to 65 million years old in the London basin and East Anglia.

This great geological range gives Britain its remarkable diversity of landscape. As soon as men started building with local stone rather than timber, regional towns and villages began to look very different from one another. Where clays predominate, for example, bricks are manufactured; deep red sandstones are used in Devon and Cornwall; and cottages of hard grey granite withstand the equally hard weather of the Scottish Highlands.

Large areas of Wales, western England, northern Scotland and Ireland are composed of rocks that are mainly igneous or metamorphic (volcanic or crystalline). Most surface rocks in Britain, including those of the Cotswolds, are sedimentary, or formed of layers of deposited fragments. The sediment was generally laid down in water – either in ancient seas or at the mouths of rivers – and might consist of mud, sand, or material derived from living organisms. Limestones are rich in the latter, containing a large proportion of fragments of shell from primeval creatures. Where the whole shell or body of the animal is preserved it is recognized as a fossil, but in a sense the entire stone is fossilized life.

Though to some it may seem simply romantic, to others it is profoundly satisfying to live in a house made of a material which was once alive. Nobody has conveyed this better than J. Arthur Gibbs in his book *A Cotswold Village* (1909):

A very wonderful matter it certainly is that the stone in which the whole history of the country-side is writ, not only in rolling downs and limestone streams, but even in church, tithe-barn, farm, and cottage, as well as in the walls and the roads and the very dust that blows upon them, should be nothing more nor less than a mass of dead animals that lived generation after generation, thousands of years ago, at the bottom of the sea.

The Cotswolds constitute the highest part of the limestone belt which straddles England from the coast of Dorset in the south-west to Lincolnshire in the north-east (see diagram). This limestone belt was created during the Jurassic Period from about 195 to 140 million years ago. There are, however, older limestones in Britain, mainly formed in the Carboniferous Period between 345 and 280 million years ago. A feature of older limestone areas, such as the Mendips or the Yorkshire moors, is 'karst' scenery, typically containing underground caverns with stalactites and stalagmites caused by limestone dissolving in the ever-present water.

There are several ways of estimating the age of rocks, but in limestone it is the remnants of life forms which provide many of the clues. Indeed, it was the amount and variety of fossils in Cotswold stone which gave rise to

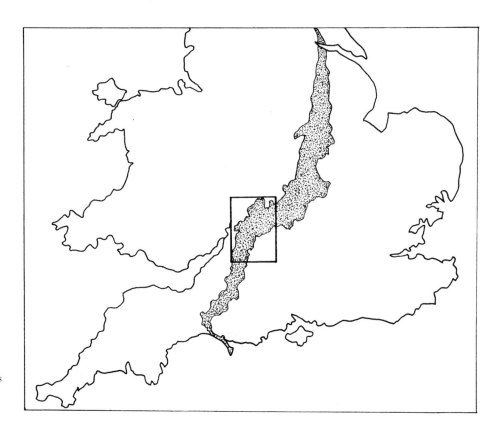

The Jurassic limestone belt extends across England from Dorset to Lincolnshire. The inset box indicates the Cotswold hills, as detailed on page 28.

the science of 'bio-stratigraphy', or the relative dating of rock layers by life forms. This was originated by 'the father of geology', William Smith (1769–1839), an engineer and surveyor born in the village of Churchill in the Oxfordshire Cotswolds. During the course of his work near Bath he noticed that stone taken from different levels in the ground contained specific fossils, always occurring in the same order or succession. He combined this observation with another – that the succession of species was consistent throughout (and beyond) the Cotswolds, although the rock layers were not necessarily from the same depth. Thus he was eventually able to draw the first national geological map in the world, *A delineation of the strata of England and Wales, with part of Scotland* (1815), followed the next year by *Strata Identified by Organized Fossils*. Some of the Cotswold layers were named 'lias' by William Smith, following the terms used by the local quarrymen. Others are called after their characteristic fossil contents, such as the Clypeus Grit named after the prehistoric sea urchin *Clypeus ploti*.

Of course, the British Isles as such did not exist during the Jurassic Period, and the relevant part of the single huge continent Pangaea lay close to the equator. Warm, shallow seas advanced and receded. The main body of water which covered the area that is now southern Britain and northern France has been named the 'Portland Stone Sea', after the smooth white limestone which it left behind.

The mass of tiny marine fossils in Cotswold stone bears witness to those slow millennia of surging tides and shifting sands. The warm water provided ideal conditions for a rich diversity of life forms, as recorded by their fossil remains. Among the more distinctive of local fossils are the spiral ammonite, and the belemnite, which resembles a stone bullet but was once the skeleton of a cuttlefish-like cephalopod.

The laying-down of the Cotswold rocks was not an even or a consistent process. For long periods the sea floor might be inundated with silt or sand; alternately stretched and pushed, crumpled or split by earth movements; even raised above water level for a time, before being submerged again. All these processes have left their mark in the stone. As the sediments settled and gradually compacted on the bottom of the ancient sea they formed layers of rock, or 'beds'. The longer and more even the sedimentation, the thicker and more homogeneous is the bed of stone which now remains. In many places silt, sand or mud was interspersed with the shelly deposits for a time, leaving shadowy drift-patterns of slightly different colour or texture. As the rocks dried out they compacted and cracked, forming the natural joints which quarrymen use to extract stone blocks.

All the beds of sediment were laid down more or less horizontally, but may

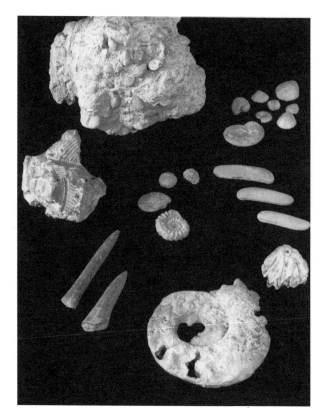

Right
A range of Cotswold fossils from both clay and limestone beds of various periods includes the large lump or 'nest' of brachiopods (lamp shells); spiral ammonites; bullet-like belemnites; the decorative imprints of Trigonia; and other snails and shellfish.

Left
Traces of the powder charges used by Victorian quarrymen are pointed out in an underground quarry near Nailsworth. Earth movements and drying-out since the stone was originally formed have created the joints, and tilted the beds of stone away from the horizontal.

have changed orientation through subsequent processes. In particular, the whole Cotswold region was tilted upwards to the west. Climatic changes and erosion also shaped the land. There are many places, particularly around the south Cotswolds, where whole wedges of rock have slipped down the sides of valleys so that, for example, a bed of limestone may have ended up side by side with a much older clay bed. The movement of the earth's crust has not stopped; currently, Scotland is lifting up while most of England and Wales is sinking, and the Cotswolds are actually going down by a millimetre or so each year. In localized areas subsidence may, of course, be much more dramatic.

The particles of shell, mud or sand constituting certain types of limestone have been individually coated with calcium carbonate, and the resulting stone thus consists of tiny spherical grains or 'ooliths', so-called because they resemble fish roe; it is known as oolite (correctly pronounced 'o-olite' rather than 'ooh-lite'). Because oolitic limestone is so prevalent in the Cotswolds, the whole formation was called The Oolite in the past. The ooliths are stuck together with different types of 'cement' or matrix, and this affects their appearance and use. Limestones which contain a highly crystalline or 'sparry' matrix are more durable, and so are used in walling, for example. Clayey or 'argillaceous' limestones, commonly known as marls (but not the same as the older – Triassic – rocks called Keuper Marls) may be too soft for building. A high sand content, on the other hand, often adds useful strength.

Any stone has several basic qualities which are fundamental to its potential use in building. These include porosity, colour, strength and texture. In Cotswold stone the latter may vary considerably according to the different types, and even within one quarry. Much Cotswold oolite is coarse in texture – the particles can be seen with the naked eye – and therefore will not take much of a polish. Harder, more finely grained varieties which can be polished may be known locally as 'marble'. Stone texture is also reflected in common names such as 'weatherstone', 'ragstone' and 'grit'. The strength of the stone – its resistance to the forces of tension, compression and shearing, and erosion – also varies widely, but is of crucial importance in building.

The colour of Cotswold stone is a subject to tax the descriptive talents of poets and painters. To a geologist, however, the characteristic golden tones are due mainly to the presence of limonite, an iron oxide. Where this is strong the stone may be known as 'ironstone', although this common term can cover many different geological compositions. Small quartz crystals (which may form as much as 17 per cent of the stone in the southern fringe of the Cotswolds) add a reflective sparkle to the appearance. An important factor is the way in which the original stone colour changes, often considerably, when exposed to the weather for a long time.

A journey from south to north through the Cotswolds will reveal the variety of stone colours in building: from the cream, silver-grey and honey of Painswick or Minchinhampton, increasingly blonde on blonde through Guiting and Stow, to the golden, russet and even ginger tones of Chipping Campden. Together with the uneven colour effects of weathering, the mottling of green, brown, yellow and white lichens, and the different reflective properties of each stone, the resulting palette is never the same from one hour to the next, but always harmonious.

Oolitic limestone is highly porous, which renders it 'soft' and easily worked when newly extracted. The degree of porosity depends on the relative quantity, and size, of the spaces between the oolites and the binding matrix. While the stone lies underground, these microscopic spaces are filled with water, rich in dissolved minerals and known as 'quarry sap'. The rate at which this natural moisture is lost on drying out is an important factor in stone working.

Varieties of Cotswold Stone

The succession of different layers of stone in the Cotswolds can vary considerably from one locality to another, and the range of local names for the stone of each area also adds to the potential confusion. The following description and table can therefore provide no more than a basic guide to the Cotswold strata.

The underlying rock strata of the Cotswolds are, of course, the oldest, dating from the first appearance of Jurassic ammonites about 180 to 190 million years ago. The Lower, Middle and Upper Lias consist predominantly of clays, interspersed with shallow limestone beds and sandstones. They are seen on the surface at a few places: one of the best is at the old Tuffley brick quarry on Robins Wood Hill near Gloucester. (This hill and the neighbouring Churchdown Hill are prominent 'outliers' of the Cotswold scarp, separated from it by ancient processes of erosion.) The Lower Lias extends across the Severn Vale to the much older rocks of the Forest of Dean and Wales.

The Lias clays below the Cotswold hills are relevant less to building construction than to the contours of the landscape and the choice of site for settlements. Clay is easily eroded, but there is a layer of marlstone between the Middle and Upper Lias which is more durable. The hard marlstone tends to form a plateau at about 400 ft (120 m) above sea level, particularly pronounced at the southern flank of the escarpment, as at Stinchcombe. Where porous limestone rests upon impervious clays, water seeks to escape in the form of springs, forming a 'spring line' following the underlying geological contours. Most early settlements were closely related to the springs, which provided vital fresh water. It has been noted that Saxon settlements tended to be just above the spring line, while the Romans built below the spring line so that the water could be channelled down into their domestic water systems.

Another, higher, spring line occurs at the narrow layer of clay known as Fuller's Earth, underneath the Great Oolite. Fuller's Earth is so called from the process of 'fulling' in the woollen mills but, paradoxically, the Fuller's Earth found in the Cotswolds was not suitable for this use (newly woven cloth was pounded or trampled underfoot in a slurry bath containing Fuller's Earth, to soften and compact the weave and remove natural oils). Where Fuller's Earth lies close to the surface it constitutes a potential hazard for builders, since house foundations can prove unstable.

Above the Lias clays lies the oolite, the fabric of so many Cotswold houses, cottages, mansions and mills. It is divided into two basic layers, the Inferior Oolite lying beneath the Great Oolite. The latter, youngest of Cotswold limestones, is so called because it is the 'great' stone which built the city of

The Fuller's Earth clay in the Cotswolds was unsuitable for 'fulling' (compacting) woollen cloth in the local mills. It was, however, used – perhaps uniquely in Britain – to make the bricks which are interspersed with the local stone in the unfinished walls of Woodchester Mansion.

Bath; it is also known as Bath Stone, or the Bathonian Beds. The older Inferior Oolite is named after its location underneath the Great Oolite, and not because of any lesser quality.

As the table (overleaf) indicates, the Inferior Oolite is again subdivided into three main bands – Lower, Middle, and Upper. The Lower and Middle bands in particular contain many of the fine limestones which are characteristic of Cotswold building. These porous limestones are known as 'freestones' because they may be so freely, or easily, cut and shaped. The Inferior Oolite is at its thickest (about 138 ft, or 42 m) at Leckhampton Hill above Cheltenham, where quarries dating back for centuries testify to the constant use of these deep-bedded and supremely workable layers.

The relative positions of the Great Oolite and the Inferior Oolite (shaded) limestones in the Cotswold hills are indicated here. Due to the tilting of the whole formation, the Inferior Oolite is most exposed along the raised western escarpment, while to the east the Great Oolite dips in a shallow incline towards the Oxford Clays.

OOLITIC LIMESTONES OF THE COTSWOLDS

GREAT OOLITES:

South Cotswolds (Bath)
Forest Marble
Upper Rags
Bath Oolite
Twinhoe Beds
Coombe Down Oolite

Middle Cotswolds (Minchinhampton)
Wychwood Beds
Bradford Fossil Beds
Kemble Beds
White Limestone
Flaggy Oolite
Minchinhampton White Limestone
Minchinhampton Weatherstone

North Cotswolds
Hampden Marley
Taynton Limestone
Sharps Hill (Stonesfield Slate, Cotteswold Slate)
Chipping Norton

FULLER'S EARTH

INFERIOR OOLITES:

Upper Inferior Oolite
Clypeus Grit
Trigonia Grit

Middle Inferior Oolite
Witchellia Grit
Notgrove Freestone
Gryphite Grit
Buckmani Grit
Lower Trigonia Grit

Lower Inferior Oolite
Tilestone
Upper Freestone
Oolitic Marl
Lower Freestone
Pea Grit
Lower Limestone

Within the Middle and the Upper Inferior Oolite are several formations of grit, hard and shelly limestones, some of which are named after their predominant fossils, such as *Trigonia* and *Clypeus*. The grits are too rough and shelly for easy dressing, commonly – and dismissively – known as 'ragstones', and used for walls, huts and farm buildings, rather than for smart houses or churches.

Above the layer of Fuller's Earth lies the crown of the Cotswold stones, the Great Oolite – hard, sometimes shelly, usually pale in colour, weathering to rich cream or grey. The tilt of the Cotswolds has exposed the Inferior Oolite along the western and northern scarp of the range, leaving the Great Oolite at the surface from the eastern side of the hills down to the clays of Oxford and the Thames Valley. The thickness of the Great Oolite varies enormously, from about 114 ft (35 m) near Bath to 16 ft (5 m) near Snowshill.

Stone slates, made from layers of the Great Oolite lying near the surface, were the traditional alternative to thatched roofs. In this photograph from the turn of the century, the stone roof of Arlington Row in Bibury is being repaired. (Photograph: Cotswold Countryside Collection, Northleach.)

Where its lower beds lie close to the surface, the Great Oolite produces the slabby, hard, thinly-bedded stone known as Stonesfield Slate, Cotteswold Slate or Forest Marble: the raw material of traditional Cotswold roofs. At best, the stone may be found at a suitably even thickness and size ready for use as a roofing slate. These naturally prefabricated pieces are known as 'presents', and they have been gratefully accepted by Cotswold inhabitants since prehistory.

Most roofing stone, called 'pendle', had to be split into suitable pieces. This job was most easily and efficiently done by frost, and it was welcome work for country people in winter to spread the freshly quarried stones over the fields in cold weather. If it turned mild, however, the stones had to be covered to prevent them drying out, after which they would not split. The slates were attached to the roof timbers with an iron nail or a wooden peg through a single hole; they were cut to range in size from the smallest at the top to the largest at the bottom of the roof pitch.

Each size of slate had a particular name, and the vocabulary varied according to the locality: from short cocks to long sixteens, from bachelors to wivots, they evoke the skills of a bygone age. The slates weighed a considerable amount – up to 46 lb (20 kg) apiece – and demanded substantial roof timbers for support. Some picturesque old roofs appear to have bent gently under their burden, but were built this way to help keep the slates in place. Another detail which may be noted on some old slates, but not on new ones, is edges cut at a slant to interlock with one another, rather than being squared-off or V-shaped, as they are today. This can only be done when the slate is worked flat rather than upright – a harder task for the slater, as the stone is more likely to break.

The production of stone slates in the Cotswolds has diminished considerably, but it continues, and there are signs of recovery in the industry. Stone slates are also produced further north along the limestone belt, particularly in Northamptonshire – Collyweston Slates – and some are now imported from France. Inevitably, the value of old, used, stone slates has risen considerably. They are usually sold by the 'square' – 10 ft (3 m) square of slates. (However attractive they look, ranged in rows like giant playing cards, the buyer of old slates would be wise to check that those in the middle and back of the rows are as sound as those that first meet the eye.) The decline in this rural industry has led to the production of not entirely appropriate modern imitation-stone slates; and to the even less desirable practice of removing stone slates from old farm buildings, which are then left to disintegrate. There are also instances of 'daylight robbery' of whole roofs of old stone, part of the deplorable modern trade in plundered heritage features.

Within the Great Oolite there are many local variations of depth, texture and colour, producing stones which are generally known by the name of the relevant quarry, especially around Bath: Box Ground, Combe Down, Monk's Park, and so on. Further north-east are the now almost entirely disused quarries of the Windrush valley, including Taynton, Barrington, Burford and Upton. Among them are some of the most attractive building freestones to be found anywhere in the world. In some places the Great Oolite is not very deep, and a quarry will also produce stone from the Inferior Oolite beneath. Depending on the type and location, either Great or Inferior may have the best building characteristics, but it is rare for a single quarry to produce good quality from both levels of oolite.

Quarrying

The history of Cotswold stone quarrying is ancient and fascinating, but can be no more than outlined here. The story begins long before records were

Old stone slates were made in a wide range of sizes, the smallest being placed at the top of the roof – as on this conversion of a Nailsworth woollen mill. This irregularity of size contributes to the characteristic visual proportions of a traditional Cotswold roof.

A candle glimmers in the profound darkness of an underground stone quarry. Smoke-blackened ledges indent the quarry face where candles (originally made of tallow), and subsequently paraffin or benzoline lamps, were burned. After the First World War acetylene lamps were introduced; electric lighting is a recent amenity in modern working quarries.

kept – back, as some would say, in the Stone Age. While that name is often used condescendingly to evoke a brutishly primitive simplicity, the use of stone in prehistory was actually quite sophisticated – the average neolithic tribesman knew a good deal more about stone than does the suburban tribesman of today.

Naturally, the stone found at the surface was the first to be quarried, and where it naturally split into large blocks on cliff faces and hillsides it was easy to convert into building stones. Following the deposits of smooth, easily cut stone – freestone – men started to make tunnels and underground chambers; although often called stone mines, these are properly known as underground quarries in the Cotswolds. Quarrying thus developed from prehistoric burrowings to the narrow and unstable tunnels of seventeenth- to nineteenth-century underground quarries, and ultimately to the lofty subterranean spaces of today's huge stone quarries, such as Monk's Park near Bath.

For many centuries, through the Middle Ages to the Industrial Revolution, quarrying was limited to what could be reached, cut and moved by men with ropes and hand tools. Although it was slow, hard and dangerous work, it provided the fabric for enduring wonders such as cathedrals, castles and colleges, which modern stone technology has not surpassed. The invention of machinery to drill, cut and hoist the stone brought about the proliferation of stone building of the nineteenth century.

A decline in quarrying came about during this century, with the widespread replacement of stone by concrete and other fabricated building materials; increased manpower costs; and huge advances in mechanization. In recent decades, conservation of the natural environment (quarries are considered to be ugly, noisy and dirty) has conflicted with conservation of the built environment (real stone and traditional skills are increasingly preferred to modern masonry replacements and technology). Distant factors such as economic forces and safety legislation seem to preclude the kind of small-scale quarrying which created the built environment of the Cotswolds; and the relevant skills have almost died out. But the revival of a local stone industry is not entirely impossible; with careful management there are no real reasons why it should not be economic, environmentally responsible, and beneficial to the general community.

Although there were hundreds of quarries, large and small, throughout the Cotswold hills, few can still be seen today, and working quarries outside the Bath area can now be counted on one's fingers (see Appendix 2). Some old quarries are marked on large-scale maps, and old place-names including 'stone' or 'quar' also give clues. Some quarries were no more than a hollow in a field – often marked, and datable, by the trees left to grow inside it – or a rough recess bitten into a hillside, now masked by ivy and brambles.

Access to old underground quarries is usually forbidden or strictly limited, sometimes for the sake of protected bat populations, but usually due to the danger of rock falls or slipping. In addition, it is terribly easy to get lost in an underground quarry. Even with plenty of lights and maps (if available), the winding terraces soon look the same and dispel any sense of direction in an unfamiliar visitor. If light and sound are extinguished, the darkness is almost solid and the silence so profound that all one can hear is the blood rushing through one's own head. Wise visitors only venture into an underground quarry with qualified supervision and appropriate safety measures.

Some brief comparison of quarrying methods of the past and today, and of open and underground quarries, may be drawn by an exploration of two quarries: the Hartham Park Quarries at the edge of the Cotswolds near Corsham in Wiltshire, now run as a tourist attraction known as 'The Underground Quarry'; and Farmington, a working quarry near Northleach on the high wolds.

The Hartham Park Quarries were first worked in 1810 and finally stopped production in 1958. Two types of Bath Stone from the Great Oolite were dug here, the more important of which was marketed for many years as Hartham Park Box Ground Stone. This has a maximum bed depth of 54 in (1.37 m).

Many people are surprised to find that limestone can often be sawn as easily as wood, particularly while it is still saturated with natural moisture – 'quarry sap'. The large handsaws, 5 to 8 ft (1.5 to 2.4 m) in length, were called 'frig bobs'.

Access to the quarry is via the 159 steps of the Pickwick slope shaft, inclined at about 30° to the horizontal and descending to the main workings some 70 ft (21 m) below ground level. (Underground quarries are entered by horizontal tunnels dug into the hillside; by sloping shafts, as here; or by the less common vertical shafts – basically, a hole in the ceiling of the quarry, through which the stone was hoisted, and in some instances the men also.)

To extract stone in large, clean blocks involved the creation of huge steps between the floor and ceiling of the work-face. Starting from the top and following a natural joint between the stone beds, a horizontal slot or 'jad' was cut into the stone using a set of three 'jad picks' ranging from about 3 to 6 ft (1 to 2 m) in length. Once the full width of the breach had been picked out, vertical saw cuts would be made. The narrow, slightly tapered saws needed to start a cut within the narrow space of the jad were called 'razzers', and were simply larger 'frig bob' saws which had been worn down through much sharpening and use. During cutting the saws were lubricated with water from a 'piddling tin', often made from an old treacle tin. The resulting slurry of water and stone dust would trickle down the stone face. The healing properties of the slurry, when used as a poultice on skin cuts and grazes, were well known to the quarrymen.

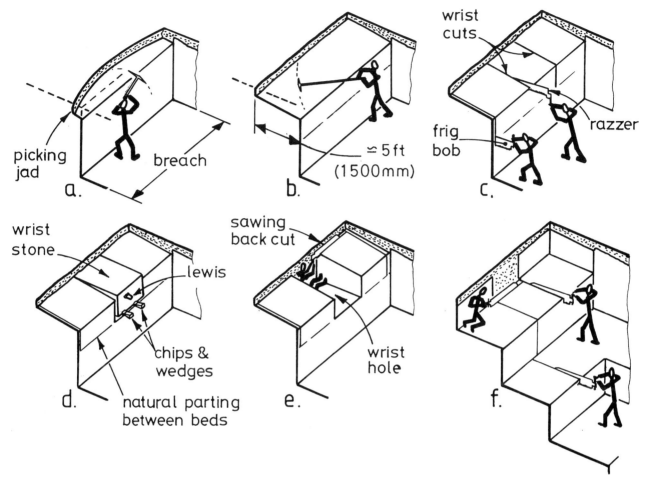

a. picking jad / breach

b. ≃ 5 ft (1500mm)

c. wrist cuts / frig bob / razzer

d. wrist stone / lewis / chips & wedges / natural parting between beds

e. sawing back cut / wrist hole

f.

The basic methods of extracting stone with picks and handsaws are illustrated in this diagram. Similar techniques were in use from the early nineteenth century until a few decades ago. (Diagram: David Pollard, The Underground Quarry.)

Wedges driven in to the base bed of the block loosened it, helped if necessary by levering with a long metal 'handy bar'. Once the first block or 'wrist stone' was extracted, the quarryman had access to make the 'back cuts' which freed the subsequent larger blocks of stone. The blocks were pulled out of the face with the help of the 'lewis', set into a wedge-shaped hole on the face of the stone, which was then hooked up to a crane and winched out of the face. The block could subsequently be moved by crane on to a trolley, held by the lewis or by large metal tong-shaped pincers called 'shears' which bit into either side of the block. (Taking economy to the point of meanness, the price paid to a quarryman was calculated from the size of the block, less the depth of the shear holes.)

In many underground quarries, the stone-laden trolleys were hauled by horses on tramways along the quarry tunnels to the bottom of the shaft, and were then winched slowly up to the surface. At the Hartham Park Quarry,

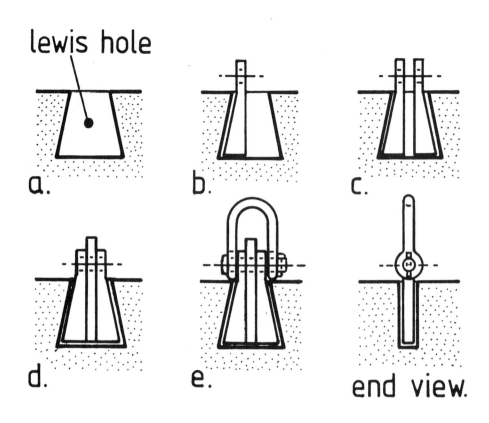

lewis hole

a.

b.

c.

d.

e.

end view.

The lewis was a simple but ingenious mechanism for removing a large block of stone from its bed. The two outer wedge-shaped irons were held apart by a central pin, and a shackle was fastened through all three pieces, which could then be hooked on to a winch chain. (Diagram: David Pollard, The Underground Quarry.)

Blocks of stone were lifted from the quarry face and transferred to trolleys by means of a crane and large 'shears' or pincers. Many such machines never saw the light of day: constructed on site, they were eventually left to rot in the humid atmosphere of an abandoned underground quarry.

two horses were kept in an underground 'stable' hollowed out from the rock, for several months at a stretch. While they were treated well enough, the temperature and humidity (11°C, and 98 per cent) made it far from a natural, still less an ideal, environment for horses – or men. Stone dust got into eyes, mouth and lungs, and its caustic properties calloused the skin (calcite was known as 'callust' to the quarrymen). During hard times, even bread flour used in the bakeries of Bath was extended with stone dust.

While mechanization and technology have made many tasks easier for the worker in a modern open quarry, there are still aspects of the industry which have changed little in centuries. Farmington Quarry, near Northleach in the middle of the wolds, has produced stone since Roman times, and no doubt earlier; shallow passages, now blocked up, were worked in the eighteenth century. Although it was run as a small family business until less than a decade ago, it has subsequently incorporated new machinery, employs some twenty-five workers, and is adapting tradition successfully to the demands and fluctuations of today's markets.

Farmington stone is a soft, coarse-textured, fossiliferous Great Oolite with quite marked drift patterns in places. The basic creamy colour can range from almost white to a warm ochre yellow; it weathers to a delightful warm, flecked grey, as seen in the old houses and churches of nearby villages.

Several stages of modern open quarrying may be seen at a glance at Farmington Quarry near Northleach. With picks and axes the quarrymen break up the blocks of stone, which are shifted by truck to the cutting shed (top of picture); here the building stone is cut, rough-dressed if appropriate, and sorted on to pallets for sale (top left).

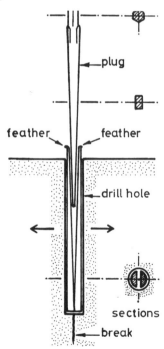

The plug and feathers work on the same simple principle as the old traditional 'chip and wedges', by forcing open a row of holes until the whole block of stone cracks apart. (Diagram: David Pollard, The Underground Quarry.)

Several quarries over an area of some 20 acres (8 ha), in beds up to 3 ft (1 m) deep, produce stone for a variety of uses. Since the quarries are only excavated in response to the demand for particular types of stone, there is relatively little waste; equally, there is no knowing how far or how deep the best beds extend.

The quarries have generally been scooped out from the surface, starting with a mechanical digger, or occasionally by drilling. Shallow-bedded stones are dislodged with picks and axes. Larger blocks may be extracted using the traditional 'plug-and-feather' method: a row of holes is drilled down into the stone, then in each one a chisel-shaped 'plug' is driven down between the two flared 'feathers' until the block splits away. With large blocks which are potentially suitable for carving, it is particularly important to know if there are any faults within the stone. An ancient test of quality still prevails: the block is struck with a small lump of stone or a mason's hammer, producing a vibrating sound. If the note is muffled or dull, the stone contains faults, while a clear and almost bell-like tone indicates consistent texture throughout. None the less, final quality is only revealed under the saw.

Stones of different qualities are used for different purposes. The most shelly and irregular upper beds may be sold for dry-stone walling or rockeries. Sound stone from shallow beds will be rough-dressed, by axe or mechanical

Some of the quarry faces at
Hartham Park rose at least 18 to
20 ft (5.5 to 6.1 m) from floor to
ceiling, and contained stone beds of
up to 54 in (1.37 m) deep. Such beds
of easily worked 'freestone' were
used to make particular architectural
features, such as stone mullions.

Young masons start learning their trade by rough-dressing stone for building by chopping it to a level surface with a 'scappling' axe. It produces the hatched textural finish that is typical of many old Cotswold homes.

chopper, to make building stone blocks of about 4 in (10 cm) depth, suitable for modern double-skin walling, and sold by the square metre. The stone may also be sold in lumps to be dressed on site. It is ironic that the irregular axe-cuts ('scappling') on rubble-stone walling, so characteristic of old Cotswold cottages, were the cheap alternative to sawing in the old days; with machine-sawn stone now the norm, hand-dressing is rare and correspondingly expensive.

Large blocks of stone are brought into the masonry workshops, swung from a massive overhead gantry by pincer-like clamps on to the sawing tables, and cut first by the primary saw into 'scants' and then by the profiling saw into the required size and shape. The cutting is no longer laboriously measured and calculated by hand and eye, but pre-set on a computer. The profiling saw can make a succession of cuts at varying depths to provide ready-shaped simple architectural elements which need little finishing off.

Cutting stone into even, straight-sided slabs was once done painstakingly by hand-and-eye measurement, and chisels or handsaws. Today, computers (above) can set measurements with precise accuracy, and huge circular saws (below) will cut through large stone blocks in a matter of minutes.

The more complex carving is still done, as it was traditionally, by a team of 'banker masons', so called after the bankers, or stone benches, at which they work. Each mason will produce the pieces which form a single fireplace, mullioned window, gatepost, archway, or whatever is required. Ornamental carving may also decorate individual finials, bench-ends, or fountains. The masons are encouraged to 'sign' their work with 'mason's marks' in the traditional way – an initial or other personal symbol, carved in an inconspicuous position.

The basic tools of the trade, the mallet and chisel, are virtually unchanged from those used centuries ago. What has perhaps changed is the status of masons. In the past, master masons might be as well-known and highly regarded as architects – and indeed they carried out much of what we now consider to be the work of the architect. In the Middle Ages, masons generally began their craft as quarrymen, learning their craft at a 'mason's lodge': initially no more than a hut on a building site, the lodge developed into the central authority and treasury of the trade. When they were good enough, masons might travel round the great building sites of Europe – castles, cathedrals, monasteries – plying their skills as 'journeymen' (from the French *journée*, a day; equivalent to the modern concept of freelance work).

Today's stonemasonry students, working at their 'bankers' or benches at City of Bath College, are heirs to a tradition of skill which was of great importance throughout Europe for a thousand years from the ninth century. The stone-dust extractors hanging from the ceiling are, however, a very recent facility.

Master masons were known throughout the country, and often abroad. The knowledge they possessed would be passed from father to son through several generations. (Because this knowledge included the jealously guarded finer points of sacred geometry – the principles upon which great ecclesiastical buildings were based – it gradually took on a somewhat esoteric character, which formed part of the development of Freemasonry.) From the fifteenth century, for example, several generations of the Vertue family were involved in the design and building of – among other works – Henry VII's chapel at Westminster Abbey; St George's Chapel at Windsor; Corpus Christi College, Oxford; and King's College Chapel, Cambridge. In the eighteenth century, Christopher (Kit) Kempster supplied the stone for St Paul's Cathedral from his quarry at Burford, still called Kit's Quarry, and worked closely with Sir Christopher Wren. In the twentieth century it is architects who are well known and highly regarded; but how many of them could do the work of a master mason, or even of a banker mason or dry-stone waller? And how many stone home owners today could name a mason, or even a working quarry?

A final, but far from minor, consideration in the quarrying industry of the past was the cost of transporting the stone from quarry to building site. Transport costs might represent anything from double to eight or ten times

In the nineteenth century the network of canals around the country was extensively used for transporting stone, as seen here on the Thames and Severn Canal near Thames Head. (Photograph: The Cotswold Countryside collection, Northleach.)

This example is typical of the most common type of dry-stone walling. The stones are laid without being dressed, and are packed as tightly as possible. At the top of the wall, the appropriately named 'toppers' are wedged together vertically, or occasionally allowed to slant.

the price of the stone itself. Since roads were no more than rough cart tracks, and horse-drawn carts could not carry much stone, waterways were important from the start. In Domesday Book, the inventory for Taynton village in the Oxfordshire Cotswolds included its quarries and the wharf at Radcot on the Thames. Indeed, it is argued that Radcot Bridge may first have been built about 1100, of Taynton stone, making it the oldest Thames crossing. Later, the Victorian canal systems and railway network were extensively used for stone transport.

Building in Cotswold Stone

There are four basic types of historic stone wall construction in the Cotswolds: dry-stone, mortared rubble, dressed stone, and ashlar. Dry-stone walling is the craft of building self-supporting, slightly tapering walls, now mostly seen as field boundaries but once providing the basic technology for all wall construction using a rough rubble. Even so-called dry-stone walls might have a central binding of clay and loose chippings filling up the gaps in the wall to provide greater stability. Alternatively, a parallel and contemporary tradition was to avoid any loose fill at all, the wall gaining its strength through the skill with which the stone was selected and carefully wedged into position. The tapering cross-section of the wall meant that each stone had a natural tendency to fall towards the centre of the wall and so, with proper wedging, it resulted in a naturally stable construction.

Random rubble – that is, stone not finely dressed or laid in courses – was used for most dry-stone walling. A more fancy variant, requiring dressed stone often of slightly greater bed depth, is the coursed dry-stone wall. These are very rare, and are usually only found near the escarpment, where dressed stone was readily available. The stone used would be off-cuts and other scrap left over after larger architectural elements or ashlar stones had been produced.

Although many cottages and fine houses were originally built using dry-stone methods, only farm buildings still survive in this condition. The technique of using up whatever material came to hand as a packing within the depth of the wall was also used in most mortared rubble walling, the most common form of Cotswold walling used on cottages and larger houses.

Mortared rubble walling might be coursed or uncoursed, and was not generally tapered in section like dry-stone walling. The fill was a very weak mix of clay and loose stone and rarely incorporated any lime to strengthen it. The result is a potential weakness in the wall, especially if it is not kept well pointed with lime mortar. Despite its widespread use, lime putty was in much shorter supply than clay and fine stone brash, so was only used where its

Some of the stones in this dry-stone wall near Paganhill have been dressed and laid in courses, but part of the wall has been built without coursing. Embedded in the wall is an old milestone.

Most Cotswold farm buildings had dry-stone walls, such as this one at Kineton. Even this type of mortar-free wall could support the weight of a heavy stone slate roof.

weather-protection properties were of value. In the depth of the wall, the natural stiffening of clay was usually sufficient to bind the wall together, but externally the stronger material was needed.

Walls were built with the stones aligned to provide reasonably smooth surfaces on the faces, with the irregular 'tails' projecting back haphazardly into the depth of the wall. There were no 'through stones', and the only tying-together of inner and outer wall faces was where dressed stones bound the structure together at door and window openings, or at corners where large squared and tightly jointed 'quoins' were used.

A random rubble wall relies on being held firmly in place by these dressed elements, and can easily spring apart in a very destructive manner if tampered with. It is often very difficult to limit the amount of dismantling that becomes necessary when a new window or door opening is built into an old wall, because of the extensive collapse of masonry that is inadvertently set in train.

The functional origin of the large stone quoins found on most Cotswold buildings is rarely understood. With their weak rubble fills and flexible but durable lime mortars, rubble walls require structural restraint. They take up uneven ground settlement, twisting to give a building a characteristically 'tired' appearance. The quoins are the key to holding this movement in check, their tight, inflexible joints providing rigidity at the corners of the

Here shown under construction, mortared walling involves the same type of stone as is used in dry-stone walls. The outer facing stones are being laid on a lime bedding mortar and carefully arranged to provide as smooth a face to the wall as possible, while other stones are used to pack the centre.

building. Mid-wall rigidity is provided by the dressed window- and door-surrounds.

In many parts of the Cotswolds, dressed and coursed stone walls are common, often with tighter joints than on random rubble. This was high-quality work, and it is only rarely possible to see such craftsmanship today. All the stones for this type of walling would be hand-dressed, the uneven texturing of the face often being provided by axing or chopping the stone. It was a very time-consuming job and today, with mechanically sawn stone in general production, a similar although far less refined effect is produced by roughing up pieces of regular 'sawn six sides' stone.

Another form of dressed and coursed stonework is called 'rangework'. It has joints as fine as ashlar but is laid to smaller course heights; the stones are also much shorter. It was a sort of 'poor man's ashlar', and was much used in the nineteenth century when traditionally hand-dressed, coursed rubble work was even then becoming a lost art. Rangework is in some demand today, and several quarries are prepared to supply this type of masonry, well suited to modern industrialized methods.

Larger dressed stone, with bed heights of 10 to 16 in (250 to 400 mm), is used in 'ashlar' construction. This is the fourth type of Cotswold stone walling, and is very rare except on domestic buildings, or the best of the tithe barns. There are two variants of this type of masonry: it may be solid ashlar, where the whole block runs right through the wall from face to face; but the much more common method is for the ashlar outer face to be built against an inner rubble-stone layer, the ashlar blocks varying in thickness to provide a 'key'. In the later part of the Georgian period and certainly from the mid-nineteenth century, the backing material was usually brick. Joints in ashlar are the finest in masonry construction, usually no thicker than $\frac{1}{8}$ in (3 mm), often

Random rubble walling, with the stones bedded in a soft lime mortar, required ashlar quoins for support at the corners.

Ashlar walling consists of very large finely dressed blocks of stone, generally used as a facing to a rubble wall. In this rural example at Cassey Compton some of the joints are particularly fine, while others (which have been repointed) are much less precise.

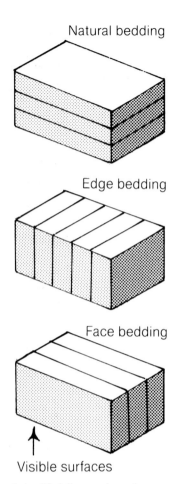

Natural bedding

Edge bedding

Face bedding

↑

Visible surfaces

A simplified diagram shows the direction of stone beds. Natural bedding is most widely used, but projecting parts of a building may require edge bedding. Face bedding should not be used in most buildings as the exposed face will decay easily.

less. As such a tight gap between the stones did not allow for the use of sands (the particles of which could be larger than the joint width), neat lime putty was often used as the mortar.

When using dressed stone the bedding, or orientation, of the stone is vital. It is not always clear how the beds lie in a block of stone: wetting it may help to reveal the faint drift patterns. As has already been described, stone is created over a long period of time, and is built up by a gradual process. This results in a series of layers which can, in certain circumstances, split apart. Stone should normally be laid in the building in its 'natural bed', that is, arranged the same way up as when it was formed. In principle, the bedding plane should be at right-angles to the main thrust of weight, so the stone beds in an arch will be in a radiating direction. Ashlar will usually lose its exposed face if it is 'face bedded' – laid on edge with the bedding lines parallel with the face. Projecting stonework, such as mouldings and decorative cornices, should always be edge bedded so that the exposed top does not split off, as it would with face bedded ashlar.

Pointing is the other major visible factor in Cotswold masonry construction. There are three obvious methods that can be employed: the mortar can be recessed into the joint; it can be brought forward proud of the joint; or it can be finished level with the general surface of the stone. Where the stone is well dressed with sharp corners ('arrises'), a flush joint can be very neat, and certainly was much used in the highest quality masonry. Ashlar always had flush joints, and where these were particularly tight (as they should still be made today), the result was a smooth appearance in which it is difficult to detect any joints at all.

Rubble work presents rather more of a problem. The Cotswold mason always tried to avoid creating any ledges where water could collect and freeze in the winter, since such frost action can split off the face of the stone, leaving an unsightly crumbling mess which is expensive to repair. In rubble work, neither a projecting mortar joint nor a recessed mortar joint was thought acceptable, the former creating a ledge on the mortar joint itself, and the latter leaving an exposed ledge on the top of the lower stone. As rubble tends to a rather rounded, uneven corner, the flush joint may spread across the face of the stone, creating a 'buttered' effect. In areas where limewashing of stonework was common (about two-thirds of the Cotswolds) the 'buttering' of stone was covered, and chemically blended, with the overlying layers of limewash. Often this buttering was also in a white, lime-rich mortar, and today where the limewash has disappeared it can still be clearly seen as very wide-looking joints.

The other treatment was something of a compromise between the flush joint and a slightly recessed joint. A 'struck' joint involved setting the upper edge of the mortar a little back from the face of the upper stone, while the lower edge was flush: no water-collecting edges were created, and the need for lime-rich buttering was avoided. The overall effect is more textured, and looks especially fine after a few coats of limewash have softened the sharp edges. Many of the mid- and south-Cotswold villages are full of buildings showing with this form of mortar joint, usually in random rubble walling.

One rarely used joint was projecting smooth 'ribbon pointing'. For some regrettable reason this frost-vulnerable joint, usually now carried out in a hard cement mortar, has become fashionable with builders and home-owners alike. The resulting angular 'crazy paving' effect is hostile to both the architectural appearance and the fabric of Cotswold stone homes.

With the advent of the first mechanized quarry saws in the early nineteenth century, increasing production of stone to standard bed heights provided a coursed stonework that gives buildings of this period an easily discernible character. The regularity of the masonry is quite unlike the finely dressed and coursed work of the seventeenth and eighteenth centuries, and the dressing seems to lack any finesse. This coursed rubble was usually given a struck joint, emphasizing the horizontals of the coursing.

It may have been an increased interest in archaeological remains, and perhaps a nostalgic desire to evoke their medieval past, that led the Victorians

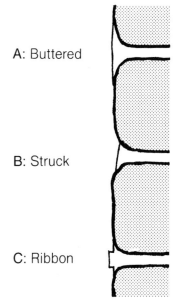

A: Buttered

B: Struck

C: Ribbon

This diagram shows three of the common pointing techniques used on Cotswold stone walling.

Lime mortar was almost always buttered, or spread across the edges of the rubble-stone wall face. This presented the smoothest possible surface for the coats of limewash which were always applied. Where the limewash has weathered away, as it has here at Daneway House, the joints look wide and pale.

Where formerly buttered pointing has been replaced, or where the walling stone is particularly rubbly, a struck or weathered pointing is commonly found. The mason attempted to eliminate any projecting horizontal surfaces on which rainwater could rest and be drawn into the wall.

to develop a further type of stonework: 'rock-faced' stone is designed to look like roughly hewn rock fresh out of the ground, and presumably was what they thought medieval people would have used. The effect can seem a little out of place in the Cotswolds, an area where the skill of stone dressing lay in the creation of an overall homogeneous texture, rather than in emphasizing individual stones. Perhaps one of the greatest ironies is that it was this rather inauthentic type of stone finish that the manufacturers of reconstructed stone first chose to imitate.

Cotswold masonry relies on the thickness and weight of the wall to ensure stability. Modern construction, especially cavity walling, operates on quite different principles, and is not easily combined with the old methods. Two skins of masonry are involved: an inner 'leaf', which used to be built of brick, was later superseded by concrete blocks, and is now normally a cinder-based insulating block; and an outer leaf of stonework, either natural or reconstructed. The structural stability of a thicker wall was created by tying together the two leaves with steel ties, initially in galvanized steel but now – following the discovery of their tendency to rust and put the wall in danger of collapse – by the use of ties made from stainless steel or even certain types of plastic. How long the latter will last, only time will tell.

The idea of a cavity wall is that only the outer leaf of the wall will normally

Today, ribbon pointing is often carried out in a hard cement mortar, such as on this cottage in the north Cotswolds. This makes the softer stone more likely, over the years, to suffer from frost action.

Modern natural stone walling in buildings is most commonly constructed by means of a facing of stone built against a blockwork structural wall. The outer face of the blockwork is painted with a waterproof membrane, and insulation panels are fitted in the cavity.

be exposed to the weather, so only that will be saturated by rainwater. The cavity ties are supposed to be installed in such a way that water is not able to travel along them into the inner leaf of blockwork, but problems in workmanship, and the occasional design mistake, have led to many failures in this modern approach. When it goes wrong, it is liable to cause more dampness than a traditional 'solid' masonry wall.

Traditional masonry walls are flexible structures, but this flexibility is hard to achieve in cavity walling. The structural loading of the latter (where the actual thickness of the masonry elements in themselves is much less than that of traditional mass walling) requires high-strength mortars, and lime mortars can therefore rarely be used except in the most skilful hybrid forms of construction. Building for the mass market today requires speed, so mortars must be quick-setting, and the skills required for mixing lime putty mortars do not exist at the industrial end of the trade. Cement mortars provide a reliable material, and are not likely to damage cement-based reconstructed stone.

Problems arise when natural stone is used as an outer facing in cavity walling. Often this stone is no more than 4 in (100 mm) in thickness, and used as if it were reconstructed stone. This widely used modern method may be storing up problems for the future, and appropriate professional guidance is advised before mixing technologies in this way. All references in this book to the use of lime mortar are intended to relate to traditional solid masonry construction.

Cavity construction calls for further refinements if it is to work. Damp-proof courses are required at window and door openings, and of course at the base of the wall, so that dampness will not be transmitted to the vulnerable plaster-bearing inner leaf. The detailing of these courses has become something of an art-form in itself, and can be particularly complicated where stone-mullioned windows and other traditional features (originally intended for solid stone construction) are built into the modern cavity wall. Damp-proof courses, like wall ties, are another potential source of structural weakness, breaking the cement mortar adhesion of the masonry.

Reconstructed stone was introduced following the decline in quarry production and its inability to keep up with demand in the 1930s. The first few tentative steps in creating a replacement material were with a moulded and textured concrete block. It was designed to bear some resemblance to traditional masonry, although any such resemblance must have been wishful thinking on the part of the manufacturers, the effect being still very much that of a concrete block. Very soon it became clear that a product incorporating stone was needed, and reconstructed stone was the result. This is essentially a crushed stone and cement mix, cast on to a concrete block core in order to bulk out the block and give it strength. The casting process includes the provision of a texture to the stone slurry facing, often using castings taken off real dressed stone. A consequence of using stone in the mix is that a stone colour can be produced more easily, and by mixing different crushed stones, sands and, latterly, pigments, almost any colour can (theoretically) be produced.

Regularly-sized castings and the need to match up to the coursing of the inner leaf of blockwork cause a somewhat mechanical appearance which is one of the obvious drawbacks of reconstructed stone. Another is that, despite

1. The steep and densely wooded valleys of the south Cotswolds take on the russet tones of autumn. Many of the small hillside villages were built to house mill workers.

2. At a disused quarry near Whittington (left) the rich golden colour of mid-Cotswold limestone is revealed beneath the sweeping contours of the wolds. The stone may weather over the decades to a subtler range of shades, as seen in the old cottages of Whittington village (3, below).

4. In general, the stone from the northern Cotswolds is darker than in the south. At Bourton-on-the-Hill, near Moreton-in-Marsh, there are graduations of colour in the exposed beds of an abandoned quarry.

Southrop random rubble

Weathered Eastleach rubble

Snowshill coursed and dressed rubble

Fine Stanway ashlar

Grey south Cotswold stone at Bussage

Creamy Painswick stone

5. The variety of Cotswold stone colours, textures and treatments can be seen in these examples drawn from across the district. Generally, Cotswold stone is grey in the south, ranging through creams in the mid-Cotswolds, and a rich honey colour in the north. To the east, stone becomes more russet-coloured as the iron content increases.

6. Two elements of Cotswold style may be seen in this simple but imposing stone barn at Dowdeswell. The most obvious feature is the array of stone slates, neatly stacked by size. The other is the pigeon nesting-holes in the gable ends, indicating the former importance of these birds as food for the manor.

7. Smaller gable-end dovecotes, such as this one at Daneway House, are mainly ornamental, and show an attractive variety of design on older Cotswold buildings.

8. The effects of
weather and neglect,
and the benefit of
thoughtful and
restrained renovation,
are evident in this
juxtaposition of two
cottages at Whittington.

9. A close inspection of
old rubble-stone walls
will often reveal many
layers of different-
coloured limewashes,
encrusted in crevices
and sheltered corners.

10. Within the porch of a cottage at Eastcombe, old layers of limewash have been preserved from the effects of weather to produce a glowing patina. Limewash was often richly coloured, using natural ochres.

11. Modern limewash in a Cirencester courtyard has a soft matt finish which complements many of today's interior design and colour schemes.

12. Started in 1854, Woodchester Mansion was a remarkable attempt to revive traditional, medieval-inspired masonry construction techniques. Its architect, Benjamin Bucknall, was inspired by the writings on medieval French architecture of Viollet-le-Duc, one of the most important theorists of the nineteenth century.

13. The Cotswold roughcast tradition remains at its strongest at Great Badminton, where most of the houses, such as this row, retain rich orange-red limewash coats over the roughcast.

the incorporation of stone in the mix, some very odd colours have been produced that are far from convincing. One recent marketing trend has been to produce reconstructed stone that is supposed to have a weathered stone colour. Often this simply looks as if a tin of grey paint has been tipped into the mix, the result appearing even less realistic than the normal, un-weathered variety.

No industrial imitations can reproduce the geological complexity of Cotswold stone, and they are certainly unable to replicate centuries of masons' craftsmanship. Nevertheless, reconstructed stone does have its uses, typically in large speculative housing estates – in something the developer hopefully calls 'Cotswold Style' – where the natural material would be far too expensive. Stone is becoming precious, and must be retained for repairs to genuine Cotswold stone homes, or for new stone dwellings in sensitive locations which are part of this area's unique historic environment.

Lime

The use of lime is one of the largely forgotten skills of traditional building, a knowledge which is being half-remembered, half-redefined today. Almost all old buildings incorporated lime in mortars, renders, plasters and surface washes, making it a common household commodity, even more so than cement is now. A delightful passage from Shakespeare's *A Midsummer-Night's Dream* (Act V, Scene i) reflects this familiarity:

Wall: In this same interlude it doth befall
That I, one Snout by name, present a wall;
And such a wall, as I would have you think,
That had in it a cranny'd hole or chink,
Through which the lovers, Pyramus and Thisby,
Did whisper often very secretly.
This lime, this rough-cast, and this stone doth show
That I am that same wall; the truth is so:
And this the cranny is, right and sinister,
Through which the fearful lovers are to whisper.

Theseus: Would you desire lime and hair to speak better?

Demetrius: It is the wittiest partition that I ever heard discourse, my lord.

In past times the use of lime was, like many other techniques, based both on widespread experience handed down from generation to generation within local communities, and on the immediate availability of the raw materials and

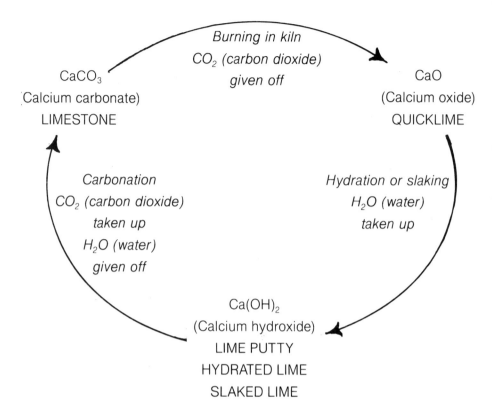

No particular knowledge of chemistry is required to understand the cycle by which building lime is linked to limestone. Lime mortar was once used on all types of building, but on Cotswold limestone it is particularly appropriate – 'like with like'.

equipment. For a variety of social and economic reasons, neither of these factors exists in many places today, and the use of lime is therefore often perceived as archaic, obscure, difficult and dangerous. But lime has many practical advantages, and was not used simply because cement had not yet been invented. (Portland cement was patented in 1824 but did not come into widespread use until the turn of the century.) Now the advantages of using lime are gradually becoming more appreciated, and its enthusiasts less likely to be labelled as cranks. With this increasing familiarity should come an understanding of the relevance of lime to both old and new buildings.

The use of lime in Cotswold stone homes is particularly satisfying in that it involves working with the natural material of the building. The use of lime forms a simple cycle, as shown in the diagram, linking a Cotswold stone house both with its environment and with its historical tradition. For these reasons, as well as out of interest, the basic essentials of lime mortars, plasters and washes are described here.

The making of lime in this country increased enormously in the eighteenth and nineteenth centuries, mostly due to the demands of agriculture. W.H. Pyne's *Microcosm* (1808) states that 'Lime is an article of great consideration.

. . . From the quantity used in building houses, walls, plastering, &c. it forms an important item in the national expenditure. The consumption of it has been also of late greatly increased by its successful application to agricultural purposes.' Lime was made, however, before historical records were kept. The earliest known lime kiln has been found on a Mesopotamian site dating back four and a half thousand years; the ancient Egyptians, Greeks and Romans all used lime; and through the Middle Ages simple kilns varied little from those seen on Roman sites.

There is scant archaeological evidence of simple early kilns in this country; they were little more than pits with a lining or mound of stone built above, the stone finally being removed or falling into the pit. Weeds and brambles soon cover such a site, and even kilns built only a century or so ago, of known location, may be hard to find on the ground. As one might expect, lime kilns abounded in the Cotswolds, and almost wherever there was a quarry, there was a kiln. In addition, many large farms would have had their own small field kiln. Unfortunately, there are hardly any lime kilns still maintained in good condition in the Cotswolds. It is easy to imagine, looking at the example shown here, how easy it must have been for unwary people – attracted, perhaps, by the warmth arising from it – to fall into a lime kiln and be injured, or even killed.

Since quicklime is too dangerous and easily degraded to be transported to its place of use, a considerable industry arose in getting the raw material – limestone – to local kilns. As with the transport of building stone, this was most popularly done by water, and the large kilns which remain around Britain today are often situated at a seaside harbour or next to a canal or navigable river. The burning of limestone produced about half its weight of quicklime, and it has been calculated that the average Victorian draw-kiln produced about 10 to 15 tons a day, sufficient to treat only 2 to 5 acres (0.8 to 2 ha) of land. Another estimate suggests that some 6 tons of lime putty, made from about 2.5 tons of quicklime, were needed for an average-sized house. No wonder there were thousands of kilns.

The design of small kilns varied locally, but often they consisted of a deep vase-shaped structure, usually set against a bank to allow access for horse-drawn vehicles to supply at the top and remove at the bottom. The chunks of limestone would be dropped in, and heated either by means of a fire at the bottom, or by interspersed layers of burning wood or coal. The minimum temperature needed is 880 °C, and the best lime is produced at little over 900 °C, which is typical of wood-burning kilns. The burnt stone extracted from the kiln, known as 'lump lime', was carefully picked over by hand and pieces containing impurities, or those over- or under-burnt, were rejected for use in building.

An old lime kiln in the south Cotswolds shows the typical construction of the small kilns which once abounded in the region. The stone was tipped into the vase-shaped 'pot' (above) and after burning, the resulting quicklime was taken out from the lower opening or 'draw-hole' (opposite).

The transport of lump lime is fraught with potential danger, since even the smallest amount of water may start to slake the lime and give off heat, causing injury or fire. In the days before safety measures were stringently implemented, both kilns and quicklime undoubtedly caused many unpleasant casualties. The quicklime may also simply absorb water from a damp atmosphere if left exposed – this is known as 'air slaking' – and is subsequently useless for building purposes.

Slaking is an inherently dangerous process, due to the extremely caustic nature of quicklime, which is at the far end of the pH scale and can 'burn' like acid. It is therefore essential that slaking should be undertaken only by, or under the supervision of, experienced workers, and all present must wear protective clothing – especially goggles – and have facilities for eye-washing and first aid immediately at hand.

Water is poured into a suitable metal container, such as a galvanized water tank, and the lime is added to the water – never the other way round – in the proportion of one volume of lime to at least three volumes of water. Hot water speeds the process, and some tanks can be heated from below. There is an immediate and dramatic reaction, with the water fizzing and soon boiling as the quicklime breaks down. As the lime slakes it resembles a boiling white porridge, bubbling and popping. After about half an hour the reaction settles down and the putty takes on its final appearance, similar to soft cream cheese. Frequent scraping and stirring is needed to ensure that all the lumps break down evenly.

Once the reaction is complete and the water has cooled, the result is a smooth slippery mass of 'lime putty' covered by a layer of residual liquid solution ('lime water') – reminiscent of the separation of milk into curds and whey. The putty is strained through a sieve to extract any remaining large fragments, left to settle, and stored usually under a layer of lime water, in an airtight container – such as a plastic bucket or drum with a tight-fitting lid.

It is the acceptance of the delay necessitated in maturing lime putty which distinguishes lime enthusiasts from instant-cement-users. Lime is patient; cement is impatient. Lime putty should be kept for at least a fortnight, preferably a month or more, before use; and it continues to improve, if stored under the right conditions, for months or even years. It is not unknown for lime to create among its users a respect, almost a mystique, akin to the vintage of fine wines. It certainly precludes an instant-fix approach to building repairs.

A good fine lime putty is a remarkably universal material, forming the basis of a whole range of techniques and finishes: mortar, plaster, render, colour wash, transparent shelter coat, cleansing poultice, and even stone repair glue. Provided the putty or its derivative products are kept damp and frost-free, they will last for months or years. What is not used one day can be kept for another, so there need be no waste. Being part of the Cotswold landscape, lime is biodegradable and will not pollute the environment. Lime is tolerant: mistakes can usually be corrected easily, since time is on one's side and water is the basic solvent.

If this is such a wonderful material, why is it not still in widespread use? The answer to that question must lie largely in our modern lifestyles. Using lime takes an indeterminate amount of time, and time is something to be saved and precisely costed (or so we are urged to believe). Lime is very variable in quality and behaviour, so consistent results cannot be guaranteed. Every small variation in the components of a mix, the nature of each building

Slaking lime should only be undertaken with experienced supervision, wearing safety clothing including goggles, mask and gloves. When the quicklime is added to the water it rapidly boils, popping and spitting like volcanic mud, and giving off an acrid steam.

and its immediate environment, and the weather, will have an effect on the use of lime. Good lime practice also demands thought, research, experimentation, and experience on the part of the user. The skills and materials are not easily available everywhere, and this adds to cost — although, once acquired, it becomes a very economical skill for the DIY stone home owner.

Quicklime should be used as soon as possible after purchase, as any contact with moisture (even in damp air) may cause it to slake and thus render it useless for making lime putty.

To make basic mortar, or 'coarse stuff', sharp sand and other aggregates – especially stone dust – are mixed into the lime putty, in a basic ratio of 1:2 or 1:3 lime:aggregate, as required for each particular job. The quality of sand is extremely important. The individual grains should be of variable size and as 'spiky' as possible to interlock well, rather than small, evenly-sized and rounded. The sand should feel literally 'sharp' and gritty, unevenly speckled with different colours, having some 'body' in the hand, as opposed to a smooth, or even powdery, pouring consistency. It is almost impossible to describe in words, but handling as many different sands as possible will promote discrimination.

As for the quantity of sand, Richard Neve wrote in *The City and Country Purchaser* in 1726: 'The proportions of lime to sand in making mortar ought to be various, according to the goodness or badness of the materials; and therefore it is to be regulated by the judgement of experienced and skillful workmen in each particular country, rather than by any stated proportions.' It could not be better put today.

As with putty, the longer the coarse stuff is allowed to mature, the better. Where it is known well in advance that a particular mix is required, the quicklime may from the start be slaked with the required additives. Occasional paddling and chopping of the coarse stuff during storage will improve its consistency.

To make a mortar for repointing, the lime putty may be combined with various quantities of sharp sands, stone dust, pozzolanic additives, and bag lime until the appropriate texture and colour are achieved.

Slaked lime is best used in the form of putty, but it is also dried commercially and sold as 'dry hydrate' or 'bag lime' at builders' merchants. Lime putty may be made by mixing this dry hydrated lime with water and leaving it for at least two weeks, but the quality is unreliable because there is no knowing how long the dry hydrate has been stored, and it may have partly carbonated. Bag lime is, however, extremely useful for stiffening up a mortar which is too wet. Small quantities of the powder may be added and chopped in, together with an appropriate amount of stone dust, and the mortar allowed to dry for a while until the texture is right.

Lime putty and mortars are non-hydraulic, that is, they will not – obviously – set under water. 'Hydrate' of lime should not be confused with 'hydraulic' limes, which, like cement, form a chemical set in the presence of water. Non-hydraulic lime mortars only stiffen or 'go off' when exposed to the air. This chemical process is known as carbonation: the mortar exchanges water for carbon dioxide to return to its original chemical construction (see lime cycle diagram). The use of an argillaceous limestone, or the addition of clayey material to the mixture, produces a faster-setting 'hydraulic lime'. In the past there were many different hydraulic limes produced in this country, but they have now all but disappeared, although they may be obtained from other countries.

The properties of hydraulic lime can to a certain extent be achieved with the addition of a proportion of white cement (not Portland cement or masonry cement) to the mix. The amount will vary enormously, depending on its specific purpose: it may be from as much as one-third to less than 1:100. Scientific debate continues into the best proportions for different uses. It should, however, be stressed that experimentation by the amateur, especially on historic building fabric, is not recommended.

Lime mortars are also given improved strength and setting properties by adding aggregates called 'pozzolans'. These were originally used by the ancient Romans, and were made from crushed volcanic ash in the town of Pozzuoli near Naples; but other fired clays, such as crushed bricks or tiles, were, and still are, used. Ground fired pottery clay, known as 'grog', is an easily obtained and useful pozzolan. The twentieth century has come up with two new pozzolans: HTI, or high temperature insulation material, of powdered china clay; and PFA, or pulverised fly ash, a by-product of coal-fired power stations.

The purity of pozzolans is important for the avoidance of unwanted chemical reactions or unsound results. The sand used in lime mortar must also be scrupulously clean, to avoid incorporating sea salts into the building which may leach out and damage the stonework. Finally, the colour of sands and other materials in the mortar must be considered from the point of view of final colour, which may of course be quite different after drying out.

The ingredients which were incorporated into old traditional mortars sound as though they come from a witch's recipe book. The eminent stone conservator John Ashurst (1985) has listed some, including skimmed milk, egg whites, linseed oil, animal blood, beeswax, keratin (animal hooves and horns), tallow (animal fat), beer, malt, urine, bitumen, candle-wax, and sugar. Apart from sheer curiosity and entertainment, there would seem to be little practical value today in recreating these concoctions, though linseed oil and tallow are sometimes used for waterproofing. Organic additives may, however, add smell, and encourage fungal growth. Animal hair (particularly from cattle or horses), coal dust, and pigments may also be added to mortars and lime renders to achieve various levels of workability, hydraulic set, strength, colour and texture.

The carbonation of a pure lime mortar is necessarily slow, indeed the slower the better. Regular spraying with water and covering the work overnight with damp sheeting is recommended in dry or windy weather, to prevent the outer surfaces of the mortar drying much faster than the protected parts, which will result in cracking and crumbling. There may also be problems if frost is liable to occur before a lime mortar has had the necessary weeks to dry out.

Rather than experimenting, the newcomer to lime is advised to seek information and, if appropriate, specific training from one of the specialist sources, such as those indicated in Appendix 2. The use of lime on a small scale, as in repointing, is well within the capacity of the amateur, provided the necessary permissions, standards, and safety procedures are taken into account.

Lime was almost as widely used in render as it was in mortar. It is not always realized that rendering Cotswold stone house walls was a sensible procedure, and common until recent decades. The vogue for cottage renovation has led to lime renders – admittedly, often in a shabby state of repair – being ardently ripped and chipped away, leaving raw-looking stonework exposed to the elements, perhaps for the first time. Not only does a historic building look odd when 'flayed'; it is often only perceived several years later (and perhaps too late) that the render provided necessary protection, often for a soft and rubbly stone with wide joints, which will not withstand weather. What will probably be noticed much more swiftly, however, is increased internal dampness. Just as our own skin provides a defence against infection, a layer of lime protects the body of stone beneath. Rendering should be considered from the practical point of view, not subject to current architectural fashions or assumptions that a Cotswold stone building must be seen to be made of stone.

Where render must be replaced, close consideration should be given to whether to re-render with an appropriate mix, or protect the exposed stone with a limewash or shelter coat (see below). A 'roughcast' render can add to a building a rich textural finish which is both visually satisfying and traditionally correct. It is, as its name suggests, thrown on to the wall, with a kind of forearm flick. Sharp sand, perhaps containing small pebbles or broken stone and shells, is added to the mortar with enough water to make the mix porridgy in texture. The underlying scratch coat is ideally not completely stiffened, retaining a slight

Where old render is broken and decayed, as on the front wall of this house near Minchinhampton, it is tempting to strip it off and leave the wall bare, as was done on the gable end; but internal dampness has occurred as a result.

plasticity, and is well keyed by dragging the trowel, or hatching shallow cuts. It was equally common, however, for vernacular Cotswold buildings to have the render thrown directly on to the dampened stone surface.

A roughcast render may be so rough that it appears positively shaggy, but this was traditionally tempered by the addition of several layers of limewash. Weathering also evens out the texture quite quickly. In some buildings, the

render is thinned out at the corners of the building to leave the smooth ashlar quoins exposed. Some formal houses were designed with large quoins standing proud of a rendered wall surface, but a modern pastiche of this style is not recommended. Too smooth a render is not desirable; nor is too large or even a grading of aggregate. As with pottery, it is said that the secret of a good roughcast render is in the throwing. A combination of expert tuition and plenty of practice leads to a very satisfying competence.

Both exposed stone and render may be treated with a lime 'shelter coat' for added protection. This is basically a thin, saturated solution of lime. Many coats may be applied to the dampened stone; since the liquid is virtually colourless, it will not affect the natural stone colour. The lime soaks into the stone to provide a natural 'skin' to buffer the effects of weathering and pollution.

Limewash provides a similar but somewhat more visible protection, and one which was very widely used in the past. William Cobbett, passing through the Cotswolds in his *Rural Rides* (1826), wrote sourly: 'The sub-soil here is a yellowish ugly stone. The houses are all built with this; and it being ugly, the stone is made white by a wash of some sort or another.'

The close inspection of exposed stone walls in many old buildings, especially of parts which have been protected to some extent from

Opposite
Limewash on old buildings tends to survive in sheltered corners, indentations in the stone, and under the eaves and cills, as on this house at Ampney Crucis.

Lime water is mixed in a bucket with small quantities of pigment to make a coloured limewash. After application, the wash will dry to a lighter shade.

weathering, will reveal thin layers of pigment sandwiched in cracks and crevices. Often a cottage will have been limewashed in different shades over the centuries, leaving oystershell-like trace deposits of white, cream, yellow, terracotta, dusty pink, beige, and even blue or mauve. Now that we are accustomed to seeing villages of naked stone in the Cotswolds, it may be hard to imagine the pastel palette which was characteristic of the eighteenth century. A newly limewashed house may appear too bright at first, but the colours are soon tempered by weathering – a process which is, of course, affecting the thin, cheap and easily replaced limewash, rather than the stone beneath.

Limewash is made from a paste of finely sieved lime putty mixed with water and skimmed milk (to add the protein casein) and tinted with a pinch of chemically compatible pigment. Earth elements such as grog or finely ground sand may also be used to colour the wash. When in doubt, look to the environment: shades of exquisite subtlety may be traced to the yellow-brown earth beside an old cottage! When limewash is the consistency of thin pouring cream it is brushed on to the dampened stone or render surface. Translucent on application, the wash dries to an almost velvety matt finish. Since it dries to a much paler tone than the liquid in the bucket, further coats or more pigment may be added until the preferred intensity of colour is reached. It does not matter if each coat is not exactly the same shade as the others; different tones, irregularly weathered, will produce an attractive *chiaroscuro* effect which complements many current interior decoration techniques.

Conserving and Repairing Cotswold Stone

An understanding of and respect for Cotswold stone will encourage many people to conserve it for its own sake. Others may be convinced by the economic fact that their cottage is built of a material which is nowadays expensive to replace. Either way, a little thought and investigation may well save a great deal of expensive work at a later stage, improve the appearance of the house, and contribute to an increased market value.

An approach to stone conservation and repair should start from the principle that a house 'breathes'. It constantly takes in and gives off water and air, and makes slight movements. Indeed, a house is almost like a living organism, in that it is intimately related to its environment and reacts constantly to changing conditions. As with any other living organism, unimpeded breathing and movement promote good health. Thus it is vital to allow air and water to pass easily through the house walls. If the movement and 'breathing' of a building are impeded, the stone will ultimately suffer.

A common cause of stone decay is the use of too hard a mortar. This may seem paradoxical, for, to our modern eyes, durability is important. Hardness is equated with strength and longevity; softness, with weakness. But there is no point in having a durable mortar if the stone has perished. A lime mortar is deliberately soft. It should ultimately be considered as a sacrifice, made on behalf of the stone. The lime mortar is naturally designed to decay and be replaced after an appropriate interval: but this will take several decades, probably several centuries.

In modern building terms, a hard mortar is one based on cement. Cement sets quickly to a rigid substance which is impermeable to water. While these qualities are vital for some types of building, they are foreign to the nature of Cotswold stone. Cement also contains salts and other chemicals which are potentially hostile to limestone.

All around the Cotswolds are innumerable examples of the use of hard cement mortars on stone buildings, and the resulting stone decay. The first visual impression is often of severe, dark grey lines of pointing which do not blend attractively with the creamy stone colour; but this is not the worst problem. When water, moving through the stone of the building, comes up against the impermeable cement layer, it will tend to collect in a localized area. This damp patch (as well as being unsightly) will also be prone to freezing; and the consequent expansion of the water content will crack the

Cement mortar, much harder than the stone itself, has condemned this wall to early decay, mostly as a result of frost action.

stone itself. Where warm stone abuts a layer of cold cement, condensation will tend to occur. Cement is rigid and brittle, and small movements produce cracks within it which negate its waterproofing qualities.

Another effect of dampness which is exacerbated by cement mortars may be the dissolving and leaching out of harmful salts. These may eat at the stone or produce an unsightly and erosive bloom or 'efflorescence' on the surface. The consequent flaking away of the stone surface layers is called 'onion-skin weathering' or 'spalling'. Chemical damage may proceed within an apparently sound stone, so that by the time the surface breaks, the internal damage is too bad for repair. At worst, what was once a stone wall held together by mortar will become a lacework of hard mortar separated by crumbling lumps of stone: a sorry sight, but not a rare one.

Repointing is therefore one of the most basic and important of lime skills. Loose and broken old pointing is carefully removed, usually with a hand pick, without damaging the stone. The stone is well wetted, preferably in several light coats rather than one soaking; a pump spray such as may be used in the garden is convenient. Lime mortar, of an appropriate mix, is pressed firmly into the joints, being left rough and proud of the surface; no attempt need be made to smooth or finish it off at this stage. Regular dampening of the work area may be needed in dry weather. If necessary, the repointed area may also

Before repointing, the old mortar is raked out of the joints, with care taken not to damage the stonework. The stone is thoroughly wetted before and during repointing with lime.

When repointing with lime it is not necessary to smooth out the surface straight away. The mortar is, ideally, left to stiffen for a few hours or a day before being pressed firmly home. Any uneven residue may – if desired – be brushed off then, or simply left to add extra texture to the wall.

Since Cotswold limestone is so soft, it is easy to rough-dress a stone to the correct proportions to replace damaged stone removed from a wall.

be protected from drying out too fast by polythene or damp cotton sheeting. When the mortar has started to carbonate, becoming more plastic in texture – anything from hours to days later, depending on the weather – the pointing is pressed firmly home, and the surface lightly smoothed out with a small brush.

While the replacement of large areas of stone in a building is a complex and expensive problem, individual stones or small groups can be replaced quite easily. The damaged stone and all surrounding mortar is removed, being broken up if necessary. The hole is thoroughly wetted and a lime mortar of the appropriate strength is applied. A new stone of suitable type and size is chosen, ascertaining that the bedding planes are correct, and roughly dressed to fit in the hole as closely as possible. The back of the hole is packed closely with mortar and with broken stone pieces. Once the new stone is fixed in place, the wall is finally repointed to match the existing pointing.

Assuming that an appropriate type of stone has been selected, it should take a few years to weather into harmony with the rest of the building.

New stone in an old wall is bound to look raw and bright for a few years; but if the best possible match of stone has been selected, it will in due course weather to resemble its neighbours.

Finding the right stone is, however, often a problem today, when so many of the quarries which produced the stone for old buildings are now closed. If possible, one should ascertain where the original stone came from, and of what geological type it is. Some research can then be undertaken to match its hardness, texture and colour. It is well worth saving any sound, weathered stones from a construction which is being dismantled; weathered stone is particularly valuable for extensions or repairs to historic houses. By finding out where stone from different quarries has been used in the neighbourhood, one can note its behaviour over time, and the change of colour in response to weathering and the local environment.

Chapter 3

THE ARCHITECTURE OF STONE HOMES

Cotswold architecture has received relatively little attention from historians. Oddly, while there have been several books illustrating Cotswold buildings, none seem to explain *why* they were built to the characteristic designs which we now find so picturesque and attractive. This chapter will, therefore, explore local building design traditions, and the settlements of which so many form a part.

Cotswold Settlements

At the time of Domesday Book in 1086 there were only two Cotswold towns of any note: Cirencester and Winchcombe. Although many of the later medieval 'wool towns' existed as villages, none were substantial settlements. It was not until the twelfth and thirteenth centuries that the now familiar Cotswold towns came into existence, and they were primarily constructed as commercial ventures, either for the monastic estates or for private landowners. Each was granted a borough market by the king, who controlled all such economic developments in the country, and it is these towns that formed the initial basis for the stability and growth of the Cotswold economy through the Middle Ages, beneficial to abbey and manor alike.

Chipping Campden is perhaps the most famous of the group of three north Cotswold medieval wool towns. In many aspects the town still conveys a medieval atmosphere. In Norman times, Campden (as it is commonly abbreviated) was already one of the largest villages in the north Cotswolds, second in size only to Stow-on-the-Wold. The outlying hamlets of the present town were then important settlements in their own right, with a scattered pattern of building that can still be found today. Campden's High Street, tightly lined by buildings, was a later creation, sited roughly between the earlier settlements of Berrington and Westington. 'Campden is a dull, disused market town,' wrote the Revd

One of the later encroachments on the medieval market place of Chipping Campden was this market hall, given to the town in 1627 by the pre-Civil War lord of the manor, Sir Baptist Hicks. It was intended for the sale of cheese, butter and poultry.

Witts in 1836, but whatever its social attributes, it remains today a treasure-chest of architectural jewels in golden stone.

Medieval Chipping Campden was the creation of one man – Hugh de Gondeville, lord of the manor, who was granted a borough market in 1173. To medieval landowners such as de Gondeville, obtaining permission to create a market town was a passport to great wealth, if handled properly. He planned the town in the most logical way to maximize his profits. He created a series of narrow strips of land, each of which had a shop facing directly on to the wide High Street. In this way he could get the maximum number of shop leases along the length of the street. These strips, or 'burgages' as they are known, ran back from the High Street to two back lanes, giving vehicle access to any other buildings that were erected behind the shop. This whole layout is still in place; the lanes are Back Ends and Calf Lane.

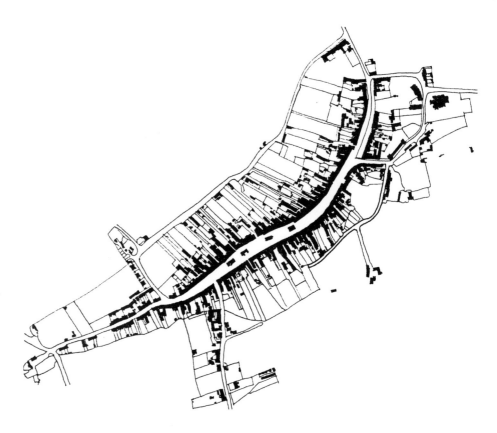

The gentle curve of Chipping Campden's High Street, together with the numerous narrow burgage plots, are clear in this plan. Towards the middle of the town the High Street widened to accommodate medieval markets, but in later years 'island' blocks of building encroached on the former open space.

It was very common for the central section of the main street to widen out, allowing space for a temporary market to take place without entirely blocking the street. This widening is found at Campden, although the later Market Hall and what is now the Town Hall have been built on it – a common form of later encroachment following the disappearance of the central authority of the lord of the manor.

The second north Cotswold wool town, Moreton-in-Marsh, seems also to have had an earlier settlement, located around the church, although this was relatively unimportant at the time of Domesday Book. The new market town was built on the same principles as Chipping Campden, by the Abbot of Westminster between 1222 and 1246, and has a very similar layout, with burgage plots, back lanes and a main High Street widening towards the centre. Here a Victorian market hall has been built, although most of the widened area remains clear, still allowing the operation of a thriving market – an unbroken tradition lasting nearly nine hundred years. The wide, straight line of the main street was originally a stretch of the Roman Foss Way, a route in constant use throughout the medieval period (and still busy today, when traffic and market combine to cause frequent congestion).

The simple linear form of these first two examples is not found in the third, Stow-on-the-Wold, a settlement which derives its form from a mixture of factors. Stow stands at an important crossing of an east–west route with the north–south Foss Way along the top of the wolds – a natural stronghold dating back to the Iron Age. Again, an ecclesiastical owner (this time Evesham Abbey) exploited the commercial possibilities, obtaining the grant of a market borough from Henry I in 1107. The Market Square in the north-east quadrant of the cross-roads is roughly rectangular, but the narrow burgage plots can still be found radiating out from the frontage with the square. Back lanes at Stow are incomplete because of encroachment by the modern main roads, although one does exist to the east. Later encroachments on the square now form a central island of buildings.

There are many other Cotswold market towns with broadly similar features: Tetbury, Minchinhampton, Sherston and Marshfield are all variations on this theme, and all largely the result of twelfth- and thirteenth-century landowners wanting to make their fortunes. Another is Northleach,

The existence of burgage plots in Minchinhampton, and the wide main street, provide visual evidence of the medieval borough owned by the Abbey of Caen in France. (Photograph: Peckhams of Stroud.)

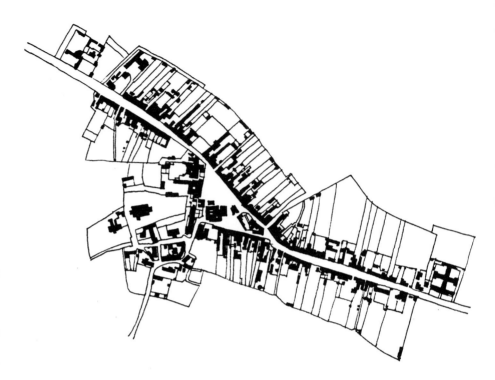

In Northleach the Abbey of Gloucester produced a burgage plot layout complicated by the need to avoid the churchyard and earlier buildings, until recently within a different parish. This has resulted in a triangular market place with a number of 'island' blocks of houses.

where the medieval layout is particularly intact and the records give valuable further evidence of the motives behind the setting-up of these market towns. The borough was created by the Abbey of St Peter in Gloucester in 1226, and information on the annual rents charged to holders of burgage plots and other property has survived in the Abbey archives. In 1226–7 the rent for a burgage plot was 12*d.*, a cottage alone 1*d.*, a workshop 3*d.*, and a market stall was 6*d.* From this it can be seen that the main income to the Abbey was from the market, rather than from residential rents. The market area is triangular, an oddity resulting from the main Oxford to Cheltenham road having to twist clear of the earlier settlement around the church. Again, the space has been partly built over, to form The Green and The Market Place. In the sixteenth and seventeenth centuries the street frontages of these market towns became fully built-up, replacing the generations of smaller sheds and cottages that had accumulated.

In contrast to the deliberately planned wool towns, medieval villages were, on the whole, built to a more scattered pattern. The relatively low population meant that space was not at such a premium as it is today, and most settlements consisted of dwellings standing in their own plots of land, straggling away from a church which was usually situated near the centre. While some villages have grown, or become more densely built-up, archaeological investigation of others has revealed that many Cotswold villages, such as Whittington, were then much larger than now. The Black Death and other plagues (recurrent through the Middle Ages) were responsible for periodic fluctuations of the population, and many villages were either partially or totally abandoned. The more strategically placed villages survived, however, and with a return to prosperity grew to something resembling their present size.

As elsewhere in the country, there are various reasons for villages being located in a particular place. Often a road junction was the main factor, especially if it coincided with a river crossing. The presence of a former Celtic fortress could be an influence; or a village may be of more accidental origin, having grown slowly around an ancient church and manor house site. The village of Bibury combines many of these elements, and as one of the most picturesque settlements in the Cotswolds it is a perfect example to look at in a little more detail.

Bibury – formerly called Bywell – is really a combination of two villages: Bibury itself and Arlington, a hamlet to the north-west, subsequently linked to Bibury by the pike road (a private toll road) with its string of cottages facing the River Coln. Bibury appears to be the earlier of the two (probably twelfth century), based around a Saxon and Norman church on one of the ancient routes between Cirencester and Oxford. Away from the church up a narrow track is a house of the early sixteenth century, a much older building than anything else in the village except Arlington Row, which also stands on this

The group of villages forming the present settlement of Bibury were all located on roadways which crossed the River Coln in several places. The lines of these routes can be seen on this plan, together with the two principle settlements of Arlington (to the left) and Bibury (to the right).

The 1770 turnpike road and bridge crossing the River Coln at Bibury, shown at the turn of the century. The placid scene contrasts with today's crowds of tourists, filling the streets with parked cars on a hot summer's day. (Photograph: Cotswold Countryside Collection, Northleach.)

route. Later in the medieval period, Arlington had become the more populous settlement. The mill (now a museum) emphasizes this increased significance, which was further reinforced by the new pike road and bridge over the Coln erected in 1753. Cottages were built along each of the roads and remained standing even after the roads were abandoned, like a ghost of the disappeared arrangement.

Sporadic growth based on changing road patterns is typical of much of the country and of many villages in the Cotswolds. Others, especially the smallest villages, were simply groups of cottages around ancient farmsteads. Newington Bagpath, a small hamlet in the south Cotswolds, gives an idea of how such a settlement might have appeared before more cottages were added. Further north, Caudle Green takes this type of development a stage further, including a few fairly large houses; while Aldsworth, near the Oxfordshire border, has grown sufficiently to become a fully-fledged village. It probably thrived because of its location on the main road from Cirencester to Oxford.

A completely different form of settlement can be found in valleys around Stroud, and is entirely the result of the woollen industry of that area.

At Little Barrington, the village is built around the wide sweep of a village green. All the cottages were built tightly adjoining one another, without encroaching on the green, which was common land.

Economic fluctuations caused the very distinctive patterns of these settlements, generated by booms in cloth production. Cottage construction peaked in the years between 1680 and 1740, and again from 1780 to 1830, to house the large numbers of cottage-based weavers who provided the manpower for this industrial growth. Land, however, was at a premium. All the lower valley sides were taken up with the paraphernalia of the mills and of cloth production, such as rack-fields where drying cloth was set out on 'tenters' to dry (hence the phrase 'to be on tenter-hooks'). It was only on the edges of common land, higher up the steep valley sides, that space was available for cottage building and a supply of fresh water was to be found. These new weaving settlements were built on common land and on the spring line, but just below the highest contours so that they received some weather protection.

Traditionally, each newly arrived weaver would build his own cottage, usually with assistance from his neighbours. The buildings were not built along existing roads or tracks since, usually, none existed. A random pattern

Rack Hill in Chalford once contained terraces for cloth-drying on the south-facing side of the valley. Weavers' cottages were built alongside these terraces, while in the bottom of the valley was a string of large, gaunt, stone-built mills. The one seen in this *c*.1930 view has since been demolished. (Photograph: Royal Commission on the Historical Monuments of England.)

emerged, with footpaths running hither and thither between buildings and linking them with the more important tracks leading down to the mills in the valley bottom.

Eastcombe, Bussage, Brownshill, Chalford Hill, Oakridge and France Lynch constitute just such a group of villages. All have extremely complicated layouts, very confusing to the modern visitor. The narrow and winding roads were made for pedestrian and donkey traffic and are ill-suited to cars. Open roads link each settlement with the others directly across the former common-land plateau. Similar groups of villages can be found elsewhere around the Stroud valleys, all quite unlike anything else in the Cotswold area.

The final type of Cotswold settlement is a product of central control, as opposed to unchecked personal freedom: the estate village. With the decline and dissolution of the monasteries came the growth of private country estates owned by the nobility and gentry of the land. By the middle of the seventeenth century virtually the whole of the Cotswolds was divided up into estates of various sizes, ranging from the very large Badminton Estate to the much smaller Lypiatt Park or Over Lypiatt, near Stroud. Initially the most visible consequence was the creation of parks, but the nineteenth century brought agricultural reform and a switch to a more productive estate organization. The farms and parks demanded labour, as did the great house that formed the centre-piece of each estate. The obvious motive for constructing estate villages was the need to house all these people. A second motive came from a desire, on the part of the landowner, to create model, picturesque villages – a delight to his eye as well as his conscience.

Architectural styles range from the simple re-creation of traditional forms, as at Sherborne, through the classical overtones of Great Badminton (with the occasional 'rustic' cottage of knobbly tree branches and thatch), to the Victorian Gothic of Batsford, Beverston, Daylesford and Miserden. Often the owner added a church, for himself as well as the villagers, or a school and village hall. The whole may be regarded as a parkland ornament as much as a living settlement, and there are overtones of an early rural 'theme park'. The Picturesque Style, a conscious attempt to compose buildings as if in a romantic painting, dominated the latter phase of estate village construction during the second quarter of the nineteenth century. In the south, Miserden and Beverston (the principal village of the Westonbirt estate), and Batsford and Daylesford in the north, both newly created to serve enlarged country houses, represent the most intact examples. Great Badminton has a series of

All the nineteenth-century estate cottages in Badminton are built in a picturesque Gothic style, with particularly elaborate bargeboards, all designed to please the owner of Badminton House as he passed by.

Many estates adopted particular decorative cottage details, such as this long row at Calmsden, near Cirencester. All the windows have an elaborate glazing-bar arrangement. Even the porches add to the interest, despite being roofed in corrugated iron.

Gothic estate cottages set among earlier buildings of a wide variety of dates and styles.

Estate village construction continued into the present century: Cornwell in west Oxfordshire was mostly designed by Clough Williams-Ellis (the creator of Portmeirion in North Wales). A great many cottages around Sapperton (for Lord Bathurst of Cirencester Park) and Rodmarton were designed by Ernest Gimson and his colleagues, Ernest and Sidney Barnsley. Their friend Norman Jewson recalls in his book *By Chance I Did Rove* that two cottages built in Sapperton around 1900 to designs by Ernest Barnsley cost only £400 for the pair, despite having solid stone walls and stone slate roofs. Jewson contrasted this with the price they would cost in 1950, when he wrote the book: all of £2,000 each! How much greater would be his astonishment to hear their current value.

The Evolution of Cotswold Dwellings

Most of the earliest surviving Cotswold houses are either manor houses, priests' houses or parts of monastic establishments. These cannot represent typical cottages of the medieval period – indeed, they are all exceptional in their quality of construction and degree of decoration. Just what medieval Cotswold cottages *were* like is something of a mystery. Evidence must be gleaned from contemporary but slightly more substantial houses.

Initially, most buildings throughout the country were timber-framed rather than built of stone. Timber was in plentiful supply and could be easily cut down from nearby woods, while stone had to be quarried. Stone was more durable, but required greater manpower to extract, and the right to do so rested with the lord of the manor or abbot. The villein would have lived in a timber-framed building of simple construction, often little more than a hut, while a yeoman's house would have been rather more substantial, often

Tucked high in the narrow upper Frome valley, this is one of the oldest Cotswold cottages, dating from the fifteenth century. It seems to have been built as a chapel, but must have been converted to a house after the Reformation in the mid-sixteenth century.

surprisingly elaborate. At one end an animal shelter may have been incorporated, usually with a floor set a little lower than dwelling floor level. There are no clearly recorded examples of these buildings, known as 'longhouses', in the Cotswolds, although they are likely to have existed.

Clues to the form of better quality medieval buildings may be found in priests' houses, some of which are relatively intact. One such small cottage stands near the tiny village of Syde above the upper part of the River Frome. The earliest part of the building is a single hall, with part of its cruck roof construction still in place. (The cruck, a common form of medieval and post-medieval structure, was formed from a curved tree-trunk split in half and trimmed to form an arched pair. Often trees intended for use as crucks had stone weights attached to one side, causing their trunks to grow in a curve.) The hall at Syde has had an upper floor inserted, probably in the sixteenth century when a fireplace and chimney replaced the smoke vent at the ridge of the hall roof. It is usually an indication that a house once had an open hall if the roof timbers are smoke-blackened. At the same time as the construction of the upper floor, the stone spiral staircase would have been constructed in the thickness of the gable end wall. The cottage was later enlarged, but these early features are still visible.

A similar cottage on one of the early pack-horse routes through Bibury shows some immediately post-medieval features. Here the principal first-floor room appears to be original, suggesting that open halls were out of fashion by its date of construction. Externally, the most obviously early feature is the octagonal stone chimney with a small spire cap. The smoke escapes through pointed lancet openings on each face of the chimney. This type of chimney is usually seen on more elaborate manor or monastic houses, and it is unclear why it was used here. Detailing on a fireplace in the first-floor room suggests that the house dates from about 1450. Another clue to the importance of this house is the nearby dovecote, normally a perquisite of lords of the manor and their senior estate stewards.

Surviving evidence of the transition between timber framing and stone, and between the open hall house and one with upper floors, is rare, but a well-documented example stands just below the southern end of the Cotswold escarpment, at Horton. Here, at Wood Lane Cottage, much of the original timber-framed external walling has been replaced by stone. The two-storey end bays of the house are original, however, with an open hall filling the central bay between. Later – probably in the sixteenth century – a floor was inserted over the hall, and a stone chimney stack constructed. Smoke-blackening extending into the loft above the service rooms indicates the extent of the previously unpartitioned hall. Ladders were used to reach the upper floor spaces, of which only one (above the parlour) was a conventional room.

In the simplest medieval houses the hall served as living room, kitchen and bedroom. The tools of the occupant's trade were also stored there. In more elaborate houses – like the one at Horton – service areas such as dairy and larder were separated from the hall, as was the parlour. These ground-floor rooms were still used for sleeping, while the upper floors provided more secure storage space for valuables – tools and, perhaps, weapons. In the humblest cottages, the habit of sleeping upstairs did not really take hold until well into the sixteenth century.

The years 1538 to 1540 saw the dissolution of the monasteries by Henry VIII, the break-up of that part of the medieval order based on the ownership of the Church, and a consequent dispersal of the Church's wealth. A new landed gentry and nobility were created, with quite different land holdings from those in the medieval era. In the subsequent period of prosperity, existing buildings were transformed and many buildings were constructed to new patterns.

Most of the medieval buildings in Burford were timber-framed, as they were in Chipping Campden and Northleach. More have survived here, however, possibly due to the comparative poverty of the town in the seventeenth and eighteenth centuries. The result is a jumble of medieval doorways, jettied timber framing, and Georgian town houses.

Some of the most picturesque and important Cotswold houses have a medieval core, but have been subject to almost continuous alteration and adaptation, especially through the post-medieval period. The result is an attractively haphazard patchwork of architectural features, charting social and architectural trends from the medieval to the seventeenth and eighteenth centuries.

One of the most remarkable is Daneway House, near Sapperton. The original hall house dates from around 1450, and can be seen as a simple rectangular block with plain gables at each end. Added to this in the south-west corner, rather resembling a tower, is the 'High Building' – a five-storey block (including the cellar and attic) with a single gable to each face. The rooms within it are reached by a stone spiral staircase in one corner, and contain quite elaborate plasterwork in a rural yeoman's version of the Jacobean style. Sunshine falling through windows on each wall highlights the decoration.

By the beginning of the seventeenth century the tenant, John Hancox, was able to buy the freehold of this house, which his family had inhabited as yeomen farmers for the previous two hundred years. Hancox may even have added the 'High Building' to celebrate achieving his freehold, and he created what was then one of the most impressive suites of rooms in any comparable house. Fitted with stone-mullioned windows neatly arranged on the centre-line of each gable, this handsome home extension illustrates the new period of prosperity in the Cotswolds.

Within a more urban context, the adaptation of a medieval merchant's house may be seen at Grevel's House in the High Street of Chipping Campden. The original hall house of about 1400 has a splendidly ecclesiastical two-storey bay window, indicating the position of the 'solar' (or main upper room) and parlour at one end of the hall. On the left, a later mullioned and transomed window with a gabled window above must be a replacement for the large hall window; further left is an original doorway, serving a cross-passage, with a rebuilt service wing to the left of that. The hall – the largest interior space – no longer exists as such; it was probably floored over by the mid-sixteenth century, about 150 years after its construction. In this one high-quality merchant's house we can see the transition from the medieval to the modern world: a transformation so successful that the house has survived without further major alteration.

Arlington Row in Bibury is one of the most picturesque and well-known rows of cottages. A popular subject for generations of artists and photographers, this modest terrace of cottages must have adorned hundreds of books, cards and chocolate boxes. The Row resulted from a seventeenth-century conversion of a medieval house and former store building, so that all

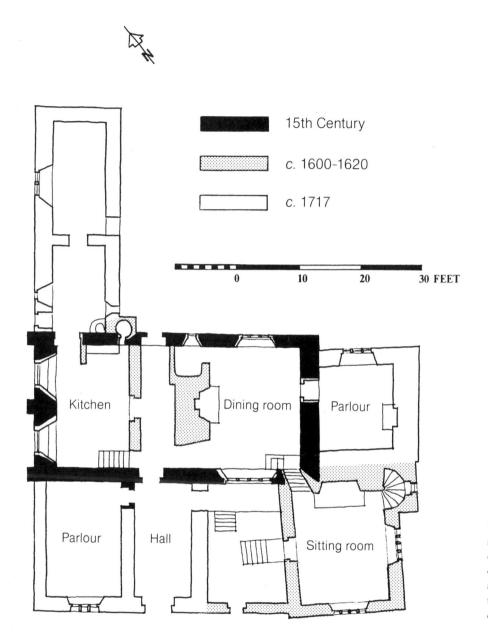

15th Century

c. 1600-1620

c. 1717

0   10   20   30 FEET

Kitchen

Dining room

Parlour

Parlour   Hall

Sitting room

In this plan of Daneway House the simple medieval hall forms the core of the present building, the large central chimney stack being an addition of the same period as the tower-like 'High Building' of *c.*1600–1620.

the subdividing walls, chimneys and windows are of the later date. The original building was a simple, long, low-walled structure, previously partly domestic, as can be deduced from the smoke-blackened roof timbers, indicating a former hall. In its adaptation many dormer windows were added to make use of the top-floor space, each cottage section being a tiny one-up, one-down size with a stone spiral staircase.

Grevel's House is named after an important Chipping Campden wool merchant. The original doorway (left) leads to a screens passage at the end of a full-height hall. To the right of that was a tall hall window, replaced by the present window and gabled dormer at some time in the seventeenth century. The tall bay window to the right – the most famous feature of the house – is original.

The standard medieval plan for the larger type of yeoman's house consisted of three rooms in a row: the parlour, the hall, and the service room. The hall was usually provided with a cross-passage, allowing access from front to back of the house. At Temple Guiting the basic structure of such a house has, remarkably, survived, together with much evidence of the way in which the building was modernized in the sixteenth century.

Temple Guiting Manor (as it is now known) received its present window arrangement and buttresses around 1580, when the hall was floored over and the walls increased in height to provide for a full set of first-floor

This famous row of cottages, Arlington Row at Bibury, acquired a variety of dormer windows and gables during its conversion in the early seventeenth century. It started life as a medieval hall house with a large storage area, presumably for wool.

chambers. The increase in wall height caused the builders to add buttresses to stabilize the structure. It is still possible to see the altered stonework which indicates the original position of the eaves. The renewed windows were to a Tudor-arched pattern, something of a survival from medieval ideas, but still common up to 1600. The simple rectangular house was complicated by the addition of a closet block, providing small rooms on two floors on the north-east elevation. This blocked off the medieval cross-passage, evidently no longer considered an essential part of a yeoman's or small manor house. As a result the entrance had to be moved, and an old doorway was re-set under a new gable. A little later a double-chambered dovecote was added at the north-west end – as previously mentioned, a sure indication of manorial aspirations.

The pointed-arched windows and buttresses impart a medieval appearance to this yeoman's farmhouse in Temple Guiting (here shown in a 1905 photograph).

Within a century or so, by the 1580s, medieval hall houses were superseded by a house plan not unrecognizable to the modern age. Oddly enough, the cross-passage was retained in the Cotswold hills long after more modern lobby-entry forms had been adopted in lowland regions. Where staircases had formerly only served the chambers or solars at either end of the hall, they now served all the upper-floor rooms. Increasingly, however, staircase turrets were added at the rear end of the cross-passage (as at Temple Guiting Manor), transforming the passage into something resembling – at least in function – the modern vestibule hall.

The hall became a dining room, while the kitchen (often located in a detached outhouse to minimize fire risk to the main building) became one of the attached service rooms. There is still, in the plan, a recognizable upper and lower end to the hall. With service rooms at one end and parlours or withdrawing rooms at the other, the larger houses developed into an H-plan with the short central link containing the vestigial hall. These new house layouts formed the basis of the 'Great Rebuilding' of the post-medieval age.

Historians argue over whether the 'Great Rebuilding' really existed. It is possible that, by a slow process of replacement, all earlier, insubstantial buildings disappeared. What is so noticeable about the Cotswold area, however, is that most buildings of traditional character appear to have been built between about 1580 and 1720. It is difficult to find many surviving

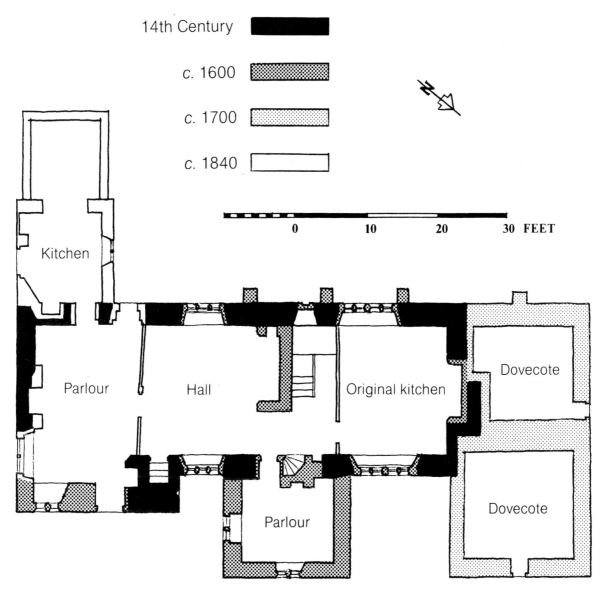

14th Century

c. 1600

c. 1700

c. 1840

0   10   20   30 FEET

Kitchen

Parlour   Hall   Original kitchen   Dovecote

Parlour   Dovecote

This plan of the yeoman's farmhouse at Temple Guiting shows the adaptation and rebuilding of the original hall. Such development is typical of many medieval Cotswold buildings.

buildings earlier in date, while after 1720 the style altered through the influence of mid-eighteenth-century pattern books. This latter trend was a clear move away from a local style based on an almost unquestioned way of building handed down from generation to generation. From this it is clear that, in the Cotswolds at least, a period of prolific building activity may be identified.

Cotswold house plans were always related to the medieval hall, although buildings became conventionally two-storeyed, with similar-sized chambers above each of the ground-floor rooms. The hall gradually ceased to be the

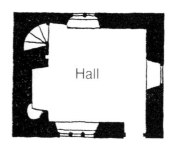

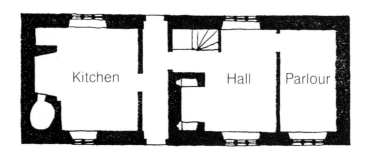

The larger cottage (below) has a separate hall and kitchen, the former with an inglenook fireplace. An example of a single-room cottage built in the Stroud valleys is illustrated (above).

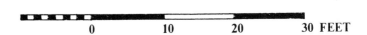

0   10   20   30 FEET

principal room of the house, although meals were still eaten – if no longer actually cooked – there. A kitchen adjoined it, while the parlour at the other end was a 'living room' containing the best furniture and fabrics belonging to the house. By the beginning of the seventeenth century the first-floor rooms were being used as bedrooms, at least in the larger houses, while in the simpler two-room plan cottages the hall remained a kitchen, the second room being always a parlour.

Many houses of this type had been built by the early seventeenth century. There is a particularly interesting group around Bisley in mid-Gloucestershire. Perhaps the grandest of these is Middle Lypiatt Farmhouse, built at the end of the sixteenth century, large and with well-appointed rooms set in a straight line. The other common form was an L-plan, as found nearby at Sydenhams. This house is one of the least altered of its period and depicts, in all its simple functional detailing, the standard south Cotswold type. The

Sydenhams, near Bisley, is a typical house of *c*.1600, built of random rubble with mullioned windows under continuous drip-moulds. There are also two pairs of contemporary gate piers, made from single pieces of stone with carved caps and ball-finials. The house still has no modern rainwater guttering.

windows are all mullioned, and located on the centre-line of each gable. Instead of separate hood-moulds over each there is a continuous drip course running right across each elevation. Rainwater gutters (a later refinement) have not been fitted even to this day.

Another form of L-plan house in the Bisley area is Througham Court, one of the most distinctive of its age. The well-gabled elevations presented the builders with a special problem of how to deal with rainwater. They provided either stone chutes, or a type of downpipe in stone, directing the water into a tank. The tops of the gables are distinguished here by the addition of

The powerful cross-gabled roofs of Througham Court, near Bisley, retain their original stone chutes to this day. The thin-bedded rubble stone was originally limewashed, the lighter residues still being visible on the stonework.

ventilators in a quatrefoil pattern, giving the house a slightly more medieval appearance than is true to its date.

The economy of the Stroud area, as previously mentioned, was based more on the production of cloth than of wool, and one of the more unexpected results of this was that even some of the grander houses had attics specially adapted to allow weaving looms to be set up in them. For this reason, Stroud valley houses tend to have high, regularly placed gables, subtly different from elsewhere in the Cotswold region.

Further north, the small manor house at Upper Swell illustrates the simpler forms used in areas of the Cotswolds not dominated by cloth and weaving. Without the need for weaving lofts, the roof is largely clear of gables, except for a central one built to receive the lower ridge of the rather swagger classical porch. Broadway and its neighbourhood abound in fine farmhouses of the early seventeenth century.

Upon this scene of intensive building intruded the Civil War (1641–1647) and its aftermath, the Commonwealth. War interrupted building activity, at least on any substantial scale, while the Commonwealth introduced an uncertainty into land holdings, not at all conducive to investment on the part of either nobility or yeomen. It was only with the Restoration that building recovered, although to judge from dated examples, there was a delay of some twenty years before local economics supported an expansion of activity.

Even quite small manor houses, such as this one at Upper Swell, boasted some classical grandeur at the entrance. In this case, the 'strapwork' detailing is inspired by The Netherlands, with which England had major trading links in the early seventeenth century when the house was built.

Initially, construction work was concentrated in the areas affected by another boom in the cloth trade. So extensive was this that many new cottages were needed to house the large intake of weavers and spinners who arrived over a comparatively short period, especially in the Stroud valleys. It is in this area that the new buildings of the 1680s and 1690s are found in greatest numbers, although many were extremely modest and of standardized design. Usually of no more than one room to a floor, these cottages were well built, with stone-mullioned windows, a large stone fireplace, and a spiral staircase next to it. Even such small buildings had leaded iron casements in the windows, and the beams often had decorative carving at the ends. Both upper- and ground-floor rooms served as bedrooms, the lower room doubling as an eating hall and kitchen.

In contrast, at the upper end of the social scale, Southfields Mill House in North Woodchester provides an example of the new building type, added to

Southfields Mill House near Stroud has two ranges: on the left, the earlier (dating from *c.*1620) has the more usual mullioned windows, while the later (*c.*1690) wing to the right has a richly coloured roughcast render, cross-windows in architraves, and small oval windows high in each of the three front gables.

Many of the weavers' cottages built around the Stroud valleys were very small, such as this modest row in Rodborough. One cottage is distinguished by a gable, but the others are plain, the one to the left having timber casements rather than stone-mullioned windows.

an existing late-sixteenth-century house. This has three high gables, each lit by the new fashion of an oval window. This feature is one of the clearest signs of that period, and also one which has been borrowed by many recent houses. The windows are arranged on the centre-line of the gables, as expected, but are of a taller pattern with a transom (a horizontal mullion) as well as a mullion – a type known as a 'cross-window'. Although such windows were common on the most important country houses earlier in the century, in the Cotswolds they were normally only introduced after the Civil War. One window on this house was later altered to a sash, although it was installed in the one place where any failure in operation would cause no great distress – the landing.

Many small farmhouses were extended in this prosperous period, and a new cottage type was developed to house the incoming weavers in the Stroud area. It comprised two rooms to each floor with a chimney on each gable end. The loft had a high gable set centrally over the front elevation. A special roof structure was designed to leave clear space for broadlooms, the hand-operated weaving apparatus then used. A central front doorway was flanked by two-light stone-mullioned windows, with a hood-mould running across the entire door and window group. Examples of this type were built throughout the many weaving settlements of the Stroud valleys.

Contemporary with these gabled cottages were two-room rectangular cottages with a frontage illustrating the increasing tendency to symmetry, and several can be seen in the Cotswolds east of Stroud. Many cottages of this period were even smaller, having only one room to each floor. In Eastcombe there are several of this type, including one, Lewisville Cottage, which has unusual and grandly detailed window and door openings to the ground floor.

Cottage designs changed little between the 1680s and the 1720s, but classical features were gradually incorporated. At first, doorways were provided with flat stone porch hoods on console brackets, and later a new composite form of building emerged, mixing grand classical elements and traditional forms.

With fine golden freestone available in the north Cotswolds, especially in Chipping Campden, it was there that these trends first took hold. Perhaps

Opposite
Even the smallest cottages in the Stroud valleys had a full gable, so that a broadloom could be installed in the attic. Dating from around 1680, all these windows have the simplest chamfered mullions with two lights. Those on the ground and first floors are grouped under one long hood-mould. The buttresses were probably added in the nineteenth century.

This cottage at Bisley has a front elevation typical of the more symmetrically arranged designs of *c.*1700. The hood-mould over the ground-floor windows also rises over the front door lintel, another typical feature of this date.

This small weaver's cottage at Eastcombe is a real jumble of pretentious architectural detail. The two ground-floor windows and the doorway are grouped under a rather primitive pulvinated frieze. The ground floor is of ashlar stonework, with expressed quoins at the corners. The plain stone band at first-floor level has had to be cut out to allow space for the upper quoin.

Clifton House in Chipping Campden is clearly dated 1717, and is a curious mixture of classical features, such as the pilasters and the pulvinated frieze, with more traditional details such as the arched doorways and mullioned and transomed, leaded windows.

the most transitional is Clifton House (1717) in the High Street of Campden, where Ionic pilasters (flattened columns) fail to reach the ground and simply 'die' into the stonework. Under the eaves is a classical feature called a pulvinated frieze, but the windows are traditionally proportioned with mullions and transoms, and the doorways still have old-fashioned Tudor arches. There are several other buildings of this type in Chipping Campden, illustrating the slow incursion of the new 'national' style, now called Georgian, and largely the result of the spread of pattern books and the newly-popular sash window. Such buildings are found in greatest numbers in the north Cotswolds, suggesting that new ideas had greater impact there than in the south. The effect was certainly exacerbated by the sudden depression in the cloth industry from about 1730 onwards. As a wool-exporting area in slow decline, the north Cotswolds did not experience the great boom of the 1680s in the south Cotswolds, but avoided the subsequent depression.

Grander architectural ideas did, nevertheless, arrive in the south Cotswolds, particularly in the provision of larger houses for the clothiers – the wealthy businessmen who controlled the whole wool production process. Architecturally, the most influential building of this period was Nether Lypiatt Manor, near Bisley, popularly known locally as 'the haunted house'. Built for Judge Charles Cox in about 1702, its tall windows with classical architraves

In 1702 the decidedly un-Cotswold Nether Lypiatt Manor, with its classical symmetry and grand forecourt railings, came as a surprise to Stroud. Many wealthy local clothiers tried to have copies of this graceful elevation attached to their own houses.

101

proved a model for many clothiers who were extending or rebuilding their houses with funds from the boom in trade. Perhaps the strangest product of this new enthusiasm is Chalford Place, a late-sixteenth-century gabled house given an entirely new frontage on an altogether grander scale. So expensive was this new façade that it was still being built when the cloth trade collapsed, and so was left unfinished.

As was usual, these new architectural ideas were first introduced on the grandest houses but soon descended the social scale to influence smaller house and cottage construction. While symmetry had already become a common feature of traditional cottage frontages, the internal planning remained as before, commonly with two rooms, one entered directly off the main entrance or through a small lobby. The Georgian era saw a change in this arrangement to something much closer to the familiar plan of today. A corridor – which in larger houses formed a hall – was placed across the centre of the house, linking the front door with a staircase at the back. Staircases had formerly been spiral, larger timber stairs being found only in the larger yeomen's or gentry's houses; but from the second quarter of the eighteenth century onwards, timber staircases became common.

The new symmetrical plan allowed for two similarly-sized rooms in the double-fronted house, one being usually a dining room and the other a drawing room or front parlour. In town houses where space often did not permit a double-fronted layout, the front ground-floor room served as the dining room, with the parlour as the main first-floor room above.

By the 1730s many blocks of town houses were being constructed, often three storeys high. Initially these had stone cross-windows with leaded iron casements, very much as installed in the previous century. Usually these were replaced at a later date, but a block in Coxwell Street, Cirencester has survived with the original windows intact. Sash windows were standard from the middle of the century, and can be seen on several buildings in Chipping Campden.

Another boom in building, which resulted in the construction of most of the Georgian houses and cottages in Cotswold towns and villages, came at the end of the eighteenth century. Again, the strongest economic revival occurred in the south, especially in the Stroud valleys; but by the early nineteenth century a moderate prosperity had returned to the Cotswold area as a whole. A terrace in Chipping Campden illustrates the change in architectural fashions, with a new interest in simplicity. Gone are elaborately moulded architraves – all is smooth ashlar, with very fine joints and classical doorcases. Similar plain terraces are found in other parts of Campden, Blockley and Moreton-in-Marsh.

Opposite
The clothier who owned Chalford Place in the early eighteenth century embarked on a crazy scheme of re-facing with fashionable sash windows, moulded architraves, keystones, and a richly detailed cornice at the eaves – all inspired by Nether Lypiatt Manor. Before completion the money ran out, leaving this strange result.

Cross-windows, with leaded casements (seen here on a town house in Cirencester) were the most common type on larger Cotswold houses until the sash window came into vogue in the middle of the eighteenth century.

Cottage terraces were built about the beginning of the nineteenth century in all parts of the Cotswolds. Cottage windows remained stone-mullioned through much of the eighteenth century, but by the time of the economic recovery at the turn of the nineteenth century, arched windows with timber casements had become universal. Some terraces had grander centre-pieces giving them some architectural pretensions, but most were plain. Many were built around the more industrialized towns, including Blockley, which was then a centre for silk weaving. Larger numbers are to be found around the Stroud area, to accommodate the weavers for yet another boom in the industry. They are usually one-up, one-down in size, but unlike the cottages of the previous boom, were without any provision for weaving lofts in the attic.

Because of their numbers, cottages of the early nineteenth century constitute an important part of the picture of Cotswold stone home

Many eighteenth- and nineteenth-century Cotswold terraces have arched windows with leaded iron casements. This is not the popular image of the Cotswolds, with mullioned windows throughout, but is one equally deserving of careful conservation.

construction. However, their style had ceased to be distinctively Cotswold, and was adapted from the new 'national' (Georgian) building style. Traditional Cotswold architecture was thus a product of the period from the end of the medieval age to the middle of the eighteenth century. Most of the dwellings described here were built by the emerging yeoman class or by other tenant farmers or artisans. With the increasing dominance of large estates, or – in towns – the new middle class of traders and professionals, yeomen lost the independent resources of the post-medieval period. Increasingly, cottage construction was funded by estates or by urban developers, and so lost its local traditions.

The Elements of Cotswold Style

There is a style of building generally recognized as 'Cotswold'. It consists of stone gables, mullioned windows, tall stone chimneys, and steeply pitched stone slate roofs. This description, however, would fit traditional buildings from almost anywhere on the limestone belt of England – which is hardly surprising, since the properties of the stone dictated the method of building.

While many similar architectural characteristics are found throughout the limestone belt, there are distinctive regional variations. For example, while the area to the north-east of the Cotswolds – around Banbury, south-east Warwickshire, and south-west Northamptonshire – has stone buildings with steeply pitched roofs, many Cotswold elements, such as the gabled dormer window, are comparatively rare. In Northamptonshire a common feature is a canted bay window (with angled corners) running up two storeys with a gable at the top, extended over shaped stone brackets – a type of bay window simply not found in the Cotswolds. So, although there are elements shared with other neighbouring areas along the limestone belt, the Cotswold style can safely be identified as unique.

Cotswold stone houses have some general characteristics in common. They are very logical in their construction, although the logic of the seventeenth century may not be readily apparent today. The controlling factor is the steeply pitched stone slate roof. Originally, straw thatch was the most common roofing material, mostly because of its cheapness and easy availability. Stone slate was more difficult to produce and was therefore reserved for the better buildings. Even a thatched roof must have a pitch of no less than 45°, so this was equally important in producing the characteristic building proportions of the area.

While straw thatch has mostly disappeared (due to the introduction of mechanical harvesting methods that render the straw useless for this purpose) thatched roofs still survive, especially in the north Cotswolds. Westington, adjoining Chipping Campden, has several thatched buildings, with the somewhat longer and lower proportions which are typical of such cottages.

By the seventeenth century many buildings were being given original stone slate roofs. The steeper pitches and the increasing use of a full upper storey give the houses and cottages an upright appearance that is more characteristically Cotswold. Many cottages and farmhouses – especially those built in the earlier part of the seventeenth century – have dressed stone tops, known as copings, on the gable ends, raised above the level of the roof to protect the ragged edge of the stone slates, and giving the building a much cleaner profile. In some cases these gables are raised

rather higher than normal, indicating that the original roof was thatched and thus much thicker than the stone slates. Most coped gables are found where dressed stone was more easily available, in the north Cotswolds, and around Painswick.

Cotswold forms were principally the result of restrictions imposed by the stone technology. The roof was always of a pitch suitable for natural stone slates, usually between 50° and 55°. The rooms below were rarely more than 18 ft (5.5 m) in width, a restriction imposed by the method of constructing upper floors, the need for internal buttressing of stone walls (by cross-walls) at about this spacing, and a desire to prevent the attic space becoming too cavernous (because of the steepness of the roofs). This resulted in gable ends of a fairly standard width, and if these two restrictions are repeated along a

Thatched roofs, such as on these cottages at Great Tew, are always more mellow than crisp-edged stone gables. They present an accurate image of the Cotswolds of the seventeenth century, when far more buildings (particularly in the northern half of the area) were thatched.

Cottages, farmhouses and barns all have very similar and harmonious proportions in this view of Duntisbourne Leer, a small hamlet near Cirencester. Cotswold architecture, based as it is on the limitations of stone technology, naturally produces buildings of similar proportions and sizes.

Opposite
The Cotswold style, with windows in diminishing widths set on the centre-line beneath each gable, was well developed at Daneway House. The windows have ovolo-moulded stone mullions, the central mullion of the four-light windows being thicker – a 'king mullion'. Each gable has a dressed coping raising it above the surface of the stone slate roof, providing a crisp-looking and weatherproof detail.

village street, a conformity of building shape and proportion is produced which contributes to a harmonious appearance.

The location of window openings is the third element of style. Again, due to the structural needs of rubble walling, windows are usually positioned as far from the corners as possible so that the buttressing effect of the return or cross-wall is not reduced. By the middle of the seventeenth century, windows were usually being placed on the centre-line of the gable end, for exactly this reason.

These three factors – roofing material, building width, and central location of windows – account for the characteristic proportions of Cotswold buildings. The style is appreciated today, and much mimicked. Detached from their origins, however, modern attempts at the Cotswold style are likely to be unconvincing unless these underlying causes are appreciated. While the architectural proportions are important, it is the range of Cotswold features, particularly the masonry craftsmanship, which forms the most distinctive characteristic of the Cotswold style.

The earliest standard form of Cotswold window had arched 'lights' and looked very medieval, like this 1577 Stanton example; they were quite commonly used from about 1550 to 1590. Strong iron *ferramenta* are fixed in the openings with leaded glass – usually outside – here attached on the inside.

WINDOWS

The window – especially the stone-mullioned window – is the most characteristic Cotswold feature. Since medieval windows survive only on grander houses such as Grevel's House in Chipping Campden, they do not indicate what kind of windows were used in the small houses of that period. By the middle of the sixteenth century, when the 'Great Rebuilding' was well under way, the first standard window types appear. They were stone mullioned, but with slightly ecclesiastical arched heads to each light (or section of window). Such windows are found in the rebuilt elevations to Temple Guiting Manor and at Warren House at Stanton. In an age when security was still a major consideration, the windows were fitted either with a heavy iron grid, called *ferramenta* (now more commonly seen in churches), or with thinner horizontal iron tie bars. The leaded glass was fixed (usually on the outside) into a slot cut in the stone mullions and jambs (the sides of the window), and to the ironwork by means of wire.

Window details provide one means of identifying the date of a building, and those of the sixteenth or early seventeenth century often have mullions with a hollow chamfer or cavetto moulding. The mullions at Warren House have this hollowed-out shape, although by the seventeenth century arched heads had been abandoned and square-headed windows were normal.

The most common mullioned window was the plain chamfer, found on buildings dating from the mid-sixteenth century onwards. A simple elaboration of this style – the stepped chamfer – may be seen on some seventeenth-century buildings. Another moulding is the ovolo, mostly used from 1670 to 1720 but occasionally found in the early seventeenth century.

The problem with creating window openings in the walls of buildings lacking rainwater guttering was that much of the rain coming off the roof simply flowed down the face of the wall. This led to the introduction of the hood-mould, a projection of dressed stone running across the wall over the window which caused the water to drip clear of the opening, and had the refinement of a 'label' at each end to prevent water blowing back.

The four types of Cotswold mullion moulding are shown in this drawing. Cavetto moulded mullions tended to be used 1550–1630; ovolo 1620–1660 and mostly 1670–1720; the very common stepped chamfer 1600–1720, and the plain chamfer 1700–1750.

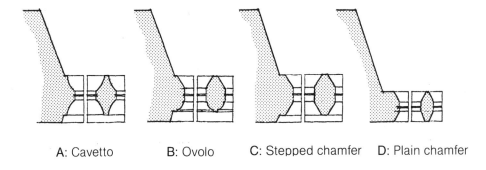

A: Cavetto   B: Ovolo   C: Stepped chamfer   D: Plain chamfer

This typical three-light mullioned window has a stepped chamfer moulding to the openings, indicating a probable seventeenth-century date. The iron leaded opening casements have the usual decorative casement fasteners.

To prevent the whole weight of the wall falling on the dressed stone of the mullioned window, a stone arch was often built over the width of the opening. Such arches, known as relieving arches, seem to be most common between about 1580 and 1640.

Iron casements were of a very simple construction, provided with integral fastening hoops which hung on iron pins fixed to the stonework. The main elaboration was the casement fastener, with a small revolving handle attached to an often elaborately shaped plate. Where they survive, these are fine examples of the village blacksmith's craft, and are worth renovating rather than replacing with standard modern fittings.

By the eighteenth century mullion sections were becoming thinner, and were usually unadorned by mouldings. In the smaller cottages, if a hood-mould was used, it often ran over a whole group of windows, with label stops only at the ends. This was a common configuration in symmetrically arranged cottages, where the hood-mould also stepped over the lintel of the central doorway, linking it with a stone-mullioned window on either side. Occasionally, where a date-stone was also fitted, the hood-moulding would step up for a second time over that, creating a rather contrived effect.

The new, taller cross-window, consisting of a mullion and a transom (the latter set nearer to the top of the window than the bottom) was common by

A later cottage near Stroud with a hood-mould running up and over the doorway lintel is dated 1735. The mullioned windows have a plain chamfer and the doorway has curved top corners – a device usually found on buildings constructed well into the eighteenth century.

the end of the seventeenth century. Fifty years later, existing cross-windows were being replaced by double-hung sliding sash windows, which could readily be adapted for use in the more vertically proportioned openings.

The sash window seems to have been invented in the last quarter of the seventeenth century, although some sliding windows were used a little before that. In England they were first used on Christopher Wren's extensions to Hampton Court Palace, and may be seen used in the Cotswolds about twenty years later. Martin's House in Chipping Campden has tall narrow sashes of the early type with small squarish panes of glass. The glazing bars, required because larger panes of glass were not then available, were thick and had an ovolo moulding on the inside.

In this early stage in their use, sash windows had no standardized number of panes. The narrower ones might have 12 panes arranged in pairs, while others had 18 panes arranged three-wide. By the middle of the eighteenth century a 12-pane sash window was adopted as a standard type, with the advantage of creating individual window-pane proportions of what was

These tall multi-paned sash windows at Chipping Campden are some of the earliest in the Cotswolds. The technique of making larger sheets of glass had not been developed at the beginning of the eighteenth century. Oak was used to make the glazing bars, which were quite thick up until the middle of the century.

thought to be a geometrically ideal shape. As glass-making technology improved and larger panes of glass became available, sash windows grew correspondingly, although still to the 12-pane design. Buildings of the late Georgian and early Victorian periods, dating from the second quarter of the nineteenth century, can usually be identified by a final form of small-paned sash windows of 18 panes, arranged four panes wide.

Sash windows usually have delicate mouldings to the inner edges of the sliding sash frames, and on the glazing bars. While at the beginning of the eighteenth century the mouldings were of the ovolo type (matching the ovolo mouldings on contemporary mullioned windows), later in the century the 'lamb's tongue' moulding was more common, allowing a slender glazing bar. Other mouldings were also used, and may provide vital clues to the date of a building.

By the second half of the eighteenth century stone-mullioned windows had been superseded, in smaller cottages, by iron casements fixed to timber window frames. This was a variation on the stone-mullioned window, but avoided the use of dressed stone. Many timber and iron windows of this type can still be found, with the opening casement hung on iron hooks exactly as when fixed inside stonework. The iron casement continued in use into the nineteenth century, particularly in the profusion of workers' cottages built at

By the middle of the eighteenth century, a standard six-over-six pattern of sash window had been adopted, as seen on this town house in Minchinhampton.

During the early nineteenth-century weaving boom, many cottages, such as these in Paganhill near Stroud, were built to house and provide workshops for the expanded workforce. Three-storey blocks were less common, although they were often built where space was at a premium.

that time. Not as well appreciated as stone-mullioned windows, many have been removed.

Further into the nineteenth century, and particularly as a result of the increased trend of country estates towards picturesque cottage architecture, timber casements became the most commonly used type of window. Some had small panes of glass, rather as in the 18-pane sash windows – usually six panes to each section of the window – while from the middle of the century onwards a new 'standard' cottage casement became almost ubiquitous. It consisted of two large panes of glass with one horizontal glazing bar between them. Each pane was slightly narrower than its height. The window was very versatile and could be used in arched openings, in square-headed openings with stone or timber lintels, or in dormers.

DOORWAYS AND PORCHES

A similar illustration of the transition from a distinctively local and traditional style to the 'national' style of the Georgian and Victorian eras can be seen in the form of Cotswold doorways. The earliest surviving examples are arched, the shape created by having four centres from which to inscribe the curve of the arch. These arches might be plain in appearance, but very often had spandrels (the shape left between the arch mouldings and the flat top) elaborated with leaf carving or – particularly in the Stroud valleys – with clothiers' trade marks or initials. Occasionally they were dated. Others of similar quality, taking advantage of the fine dressed stone available from the escarpment, are found in the neighbouring north-west Cotswold villages of Weston-sub-Edge, Aston-sub-Edge, Broadway and Stanton.

The mouldings to doorways tended to be more elaborate than those to windows, undoubtedly in the hope that a well-crafted and elaborate doorway, exuding a feeling of prosperity, would impress visitors. The mouldings finish 2 to 3 ft (0.6 to 1.0 m) from the ground with chamfer stops, to a variety of patterns, usually in the form of a vase-shaped motif.

Round-arched doorways were another elaboration, used on more important buildings but also finding their way on to some cottages, and the more impressive Daneway House. These date from the first quarter of the seventeenth century and represent an increasing interest in classical architecture, absorbing Jacobean motifs such as keystones, imposts (the blocks from which the arch springs), and rustication, and usually incorporating the fashionable lozenge-pattern of this period. For all these novel possibilities, however, plain door openings or pointed arches were much more common.

Pointed arches varied in shape, and by the end of the century were generally of a simple, 'depressed' type. Even more common by this date, however, was the plain opening with a deep stone lintel, and large dressed quoins or jamb stones forming the sides. Elaborate mouldings were replaced by plain chamfers, and vase stops were no longer found. As the spandrels and elaborated hood-moulds had disappeared by then, date inscriptions were usually placed on the lintel stone, either incised or, more commonly, projecting from a small recessed panel. These were often accompanied by the

Doorways in the north-west Cotswolds tend to take advantage of the fine dressed stone from the escarpment quarries. This doorway in Weston-sub-Edge has rosette and leaf carving in the spandrels above the arch and beneath the hood-mould. The stops to the hood-mould are more elaborate than usual, the right-hand one having the date 1618. The doorway moulding stops at waist level with a vase stop.

Right

In the early seventeenth century, many Cotswold details were taken from classically influenced Jacobean architecture. This arched doorway has clearly expressed voussoirs (the stones that make an arch), a rectangular keystone, and the common Jacobean lozenge motif in each of the spandrels.

Left

An early eighteenth-century stone porch hood at Chipping Campden, supported on elaborately carved scroll brackets. The door is a wide-boarded oak door, possibly original.

initials of the owners. Lettering was usually quite crude, with the occasional 'S' the wrong way round.

In some parts of the Cotswolds there were no quarries that produced any dressed stone. This is particularly true of the south and east, where rough rubble stone was the most common building material. Door lintels in these areas were made of timber and because of the rough nature of the stone, heavy door frames were required to achieve a close fit. These simple doors, of no great quality in themselves, are as much part of the Cotswold character as the grander and more distinctive doorways on houses built where dressed stone was readily available.

The first porches were very crude flat hoods that were added to cottages by the end of the seventeenth century. In Bibury there are several such hoods, supported on timber brackets, on cottages around the Green. They are made from very thin slabs of stone which are really very large stone roofing slates. Before this date porches were exceptional, and usually a reliable indication of the owner's status. Grander, classical porches were first introduced on high-

14. One of the smallest settlements in the south Cotswolds is Owlpen, consisting of no more than the church and manor house. Owlpen Manor is medieval in part, with additions of the sixteenth and seventeenth centuries. The stone is a typical south Cotswolds silver-grey in colour, with a matching roughcast render.

15. The later additions to the simple rectangular medieval hall of Daneway House are shown in this view, which also emphasizes the glow of the mellow silver south Cotswold stone, originally limewashed a cream colour.

16. Guiting Power is
near the escarpment, so
had access to some of
the fine dressed stone
from the quarries in
that area. On these
seventeenth-century
cottages, the stone has
weathered to a russet
colour from the original
orange.

17. This cottage in Caudle Green is late seventeenth century in date, and has the unusual feature of stone slates being used as hoods and cills to the small two-light upper-floor mullioned windows. Note the simple boarded gate.

18. The low lines and organic forms of thatched dormer windows can be seen behind the thatcher's scaffolding on this cottage in the Chipping Campden hamlet of Westington.

19. Several of the farmhouses in Great Barrington are built of a finely jointed ashlar, silvered with age. Here the two-light mullioned windows all have separate hood-moulds.

20. In the hamlet of Barton, on the upper reaches of the River Windrush, Barton House has managed to accumulate a mixture of many periods of window design on its main elevation. Some of the original cross-windows have been replaced by sashes, some with conventional glazing-bar arrangements but others in a decorative hexagonal pattern.

21. These simple metal casements are in fact a well-chosen modern replacement for the original, decayed, windows. The unimposing estate grey colour is a typically self-effacing Cotswold treatment, although some estates have selected very bright colours for their cottage joinery.

22. Barns are very simple structures, and this conversion (Case Study 6) has retained the uncomplicated farmyard feel of the building. The use of a row of five small windows tucked under the eaves, rather than roof-lights, is one aspect of the design that contributes to its success.

23. The roof structure of the barn has been left visible, a gallery bedroom has been installed at the far end, and light floods the space from the glazed barn doorway openings.

class houses and farmhouses built for the more fashionable yeomen, such as that at Upper Swell. By the end of the seventeenth century the use of classical features had spread down the social scale to small cottages and town houses, as had the increasing use of a symmetrical front elevation. Thicker stone slab hoods with shaped stone brackets were introduced. These might be very simple in profile, or moulded as full console brackets, the classical scrolled form. The hood might have chamfered edges or a cyma moulding, itself classical in origin. There are many fine examples of a variety of these porch hoods in Chipping Campden.

Most cottages lacked a porch or hood of any kind, and the plain doorway was left bare. These smaller cottages have tended to lose their simple and unadorned appearance by the later addition of porches – either of an open timber variety (in the Victorian period) or solid lobbies with an outer front

Gabled dormer windows and gabled Victorian porches seem in harmony at this terrace of cottages in Winchcombe. The sides of the porches and gables have trellis-work to support climbing plants.

door (in recent times) to conserve heat and prevent draughts. None the less, these later additions may be interesting in themselves and, while not original, have become part of the Cotswold village scene. Timber porches are sometimes quite decorative, and those of an open construction leave the original doorway relatively discernible. There are two basic types: small gables or lean-to hoods supported on timber struts, and those where the hood is supported on posts, often with a trellis-work panel at the sides and in the gable apex to complete the picturesque appearance and support climbing plants.

Doors themselves were nearly always made of oak, the very wide boards held together by horizontal timbers on the reverse side. Some very old doors consist simply of two or more layers of boards, overlapping and bound together with iron studs. An elaboration is the fitting of cover strips over the joints in the outer layer of oak boards. Doors were hung on long hinges, with the loop end dropped on to iron hooks built directly into the stone. The use of a door frame was a later idea, as early doors all close directly into a recess cut out of the stone door-surround. The long hinges – frequently of a branching design – and the casement fasteners gave local blacksmiths a chance to show off their skills, continuing a tradition from the early medieval era. Some fine old oak doors still survive, and are worth retaining if at all possible.

Cotswold cottages of traditional construction never had panelled doors. The inclusion of small panes of glass in the door is a modern idea, not found on surviving historic examples. It was not until the Georgian period that panelled doors were seen in any quantity in the Cotswolds, and then usually set within openings of classical proportions. Many eighteenth-century doorways are very simple and elegant, often with a plain rectangular fanlight over the door, set above a timber transom. The term 'fanlight' derives from the more elaborate fan-shaped pattern found in cities and towns, but few are found in the Cotswolds except on grander town houses or country houses. The stone door-surround on the better houses had moulded architraves, often with keystones and occasionally with attached classical pilasters. Most were plain, but usually the inner edge of the surround had a fine rounded beading.

Doors were made to proportions which became more strictly controlled as the century progressed. Earlier panelled doors were tall and narrow, often with eight panels. The panels themselves might be fielded, that is, with a chamfered edge and a central plain raised area. Later doors had six panels, the upper ones horizontal in emphasis (never square, as in some modern reproductions) with tall central panels and shorter but still vertically-shaped lower panels. While fielded panels were used on many town house doors, often only the central panels were so treated, the lowest pair having beaded edges. In many cases, all the panels were beaded.

The surrounds of these Georgian doorways at Chipping Campden have classical columns, pediments, and fanlights in the glazed arches over the doors. The doors themselves are always painted and are wider than modern ones.

As with all building, doorways of both the Georgian and the Victorian periods became increasingly 'national' in character, and gradually lost their regional flavour. In this respect the Cotswolds is no different from other regions, although the characteristic dressed stone was used for door-surrounds in every period, wherever it was available.

Typical Cotswold doorways have survived in large numbers, although there is a modern tendency to conceal them with solid porch lobbies and to introduce standard mass-produced panelled doors, usually to quite incorrect proportions and stained in alarmingly bright ginger tones. Silvered oak is the familiar colour for board doors, with panelled doors painted white, black, or – where there is still a large controlling estate – in estate livery, usually a cream or green-grey. As with window finishes, door colours can change the appearance of a house significantly, and should be carefully considered during renovation work.

DORMER WINDOWS

The most distinctive traditional elements of the houses and cottages of the Cotswolds are the stone roofs and stone-gabled dormer windows. As with all Cotswold features, the gabled dormer window was introduced for a thoroughly functional reason: to let more light into low-ceilinged upper floors than could windows in the gable ends alone, while still keeping the side walls as low as possible.

Initially, when roofs were mostly thatched, the simplest way to achieve side windows on the upper floor was by raising the wall height to accommodate the window, while the flowing geometry of the thatch allowed for a twist up and around this intrusion. As stone slates took over from thatch, such rounded forms were no longer possible. The ideal form of a stone slate roof is a simple pitch, with no interruptions whatsoever, but an elaborate stone slating technique was developed for use where a roof was required to turn through an angle. In this 'swept valley' the stone slates were reduced in width, and turned the corner in a seamless curve. Any cutting or introduction of other materials, such as lead, caused greater expense, and was avoided.

Dormer windows were therefore developed so that the pitched roof form could run at right-angles to the main roof, by the introduction of a smaller gable built up from the wall eaves. These secondary gables were often coped with dressed stone to match the main gable ends, although they might have plain verges if no dressed stone was available. The window was mullioned, usually no wider than two lights, but occasionally with three. Where the ridge of the dormer roof was lower than the main roof, the vulnerable junction between the lower ridge and the main roof slope could be protected by using an inverted ridge stone, placed so that water was thrown clear of the dormer roof. This interesting detail, which appears to have been mostly used in the mid-Cotswolds, seems very little appreciated today, and is often lost when stone roofs are replaced or repaired.

The use of attics for cloth weaving in the south Cotswolds led to a much larger dormer window which was formed into a full-height gable. This provided light and sufficient space for the looms, and for storage space high in the apexes of the gables. Smaller windows were introduced in the gable apex to light this upper attic level, and often (particularly by the end of the seventeenth century) these were in the form of small oval windows. The oval might be glazed with rectangular panes of glass, but often tempted the glazier to create a more interesting and decorative radiating pattern.

Boldly-gabled houses are found throughout the Stroud and Painswick valleys and many, still remarkably well preserved, illustrate the type. It is perhaps odd to realize that even in houses of high quality, built for comparatively wealthy clothiers, the attics were occupied by weavers and used for cloth storage. It was not until the nineteenth century that the industrial cloth mill came into existence; before then the woollen and clothing trade was cottage-, and indeed mansion-, based.

The full-height gables of these now-demolished weavers' cottages in Stroud are typical of the area, with broadlooms built into the attics. Note the oval windows high in three of the gables, indicating late seventeenth-century construction. (Photograph: Royal Commission on the Historical Monuments of England.)

With the increasing use of attics for bedrooms – especially for itinerant farm labourers – cottages with plain stone slate roofs had a rather different type of dormer window added. The roof dormer is a type of window not peculiar to the Cotswolds, but nevertheless present in large numbers on seventeenth- and early eighteenth-century traditional buildings. They were normally narrow, of two lights, and constructed of timber. Iron casements were fixed directly to the corner posts, resulting in a simple, slender detail that is distinctive. The gable was rendered, but might have stone slate hanging if the dormer was a little larger than usual. The sides had stone slate hanging brought round from the main roof surface, and swept valleys were also used to connect the small pitches of the dormer roof to the main roof slope.

On a Westington house the roughcast-rendered gable projects forward of the window, supported on the ends of the side framing. This is in turn supported on the extended 'ears' of the timber window-head. The iron casement is fitted directly to the stone frame. A rare upturned stone ridge-piece protects the junction between the dormer window ridge and the main roof-slope.

Nineteenth-century roof dormers often had timber casements rather than the old iron-framed pattern, but they still managed to produce a simple and slender corner post detail. With modern demands for insulation the correct detailing of roof dormers has become more difficult to achieve, but once it is realized that the secret is to support the dormer roof on a heavy window frame, and to use iron – or, more commonly now, steel – casements, then a very good approximation can be achieved.

The final form of the dormer window (a variation on the gabled roof dormer) is the hipped roof dormer, introduced by the end of the seventeenth century particularly on more classical houses so that the appearance of the roof would not be disturbed by gables. A hipped roof is not an easy thing to construct in stone slate, requiring a mortar ridge treatment which is always a potential maintenance problem. For this reason hipped roofs were generally avoided in the Cotswolds, although the dictates of fashion, particularly in the eighteenth century, were sufficiently strong to see their introduction. A good example is on Medford House at Mickleton, a grand village house built in the 1690s with many classical features.

The need to increase accommodation in traditional cottages and houses has continued from the last century to the present. One widespread result is the roof-light (or 'roof window', as one well-known manufacturer calls them).

The hipped Cotswold dormer was an eighteenth-century refinement, avoiding the interruption of the roof-slope with what were then regarded as unfashionable gables. The detailing was similar to the gabled version.

Angled glass panels can now be seen in many Cotswold village and farmstead roofscapes, often catching the sunlight and thus our attention. It should be remembered, however, that the roof dormer provides more space and is the traditional way to add attic bedrooms. When well detailed and well positioned, dormers contribute to the appearance of the house rather than detract from it; the same may rarely be said of roof-lights, which are, at best, merely inconspicuous.

CHIMNEYS

Often a very dominant feature on Cotswold cottages and houses, chimneys are usually positioned to give the building a feeling of extra strength – presumably the solidity of the building reflected that of its owner! In the north Cotswolds, with the profusion of finely-dressed stone, chimneys are at their grandest. In many of the examples already illustrated, chimneys can be seen

The fine detailing to the stonework, and the very prominent chimneys, are typical of houses built along the Cotswold escarpment. This photograph shows part of Snowshill Manor, now in the ownership of the National Trust.

boldly located on the gable ends, or on projections from the side walls. The shafts of the chimney were always of finely-jointed ashlar with a moulded cap, often with a further subsidiary moulding below. Added effect could be gained by turning the shaft through 45°, and this was particularly effective where two or more stacks were in a row. These more elaborate chimneys were generally built during the first half of the seventeenth century.

Diagonally set chimney stacks are common in the north-west Cotswolds, and on larger manor houses. This pair at Weston-sub-Edge is typical, with the two moulded caps being connected together tip-to-tip.

In the remainder of the Cotswold area, rather less elaborate designs were used, but again they were always constructed from large slabs of ashlar and with projecting caps that were either moulded or chamfered. Chimneys were rarely rubble-built, as rubble requires constant repointing to remain watertight. Ashlar has fine, relatively maintenance-free joints, so was far more valuable in such inaccessible locations as chimneys. An additional detail was the shaped projection or 'skirt' at the base of the chimney where the stone slate roof was fitted.

The positioning of chimneys was, of course, a consequence of the building plan. Wherever possible, chimneys were placed on gable ends, and usually at the end of any building built into a bank. The fireplace, almost constantly in use, would ensure that any dampness coming through the wall from the higher adjoining ground was held at bay. Other chimneys were located on the ridge of the roof.

By the nineteenth century brick was becoming readily available in the Cotswolds, either made at local brickworks or transported in by canal, and later by railway. Brick was used to replace damaged stone chimneys, or in the provision of further chimneys to existing cottages to heat more rooms. In more recent times, new chimneys have been built from rubble stone; although this was not traditional in the area, it is now often regarded as preferable to brick.

Cotswold Architecture Revived

By the middle of the nineteenth century, following the introduction of standardized industrial housing and national house styles, traditional Cotswold architecture had all but ceased to be built. Traditional craftsmanship still remained, however, and many estates and larger farms retained builders who could turn their hand to the old crafts when building repairs were needed.

A chance for a revival of traditional architecture came from a somewhat unexpected source – the socialist craftsman and designer, William Morris. He drew attention to the simple, solid quality of traditional buildings, particularly praising farm buildings and likening barns to cathedrals. Morris himself lived for much of his life in a house by the Thames on the fringes of the Cotswolds, at Kelmscott. His belief in the value of traditional skills, particularly those related to building, influenced a group of like-minded architects and craftsmen, and became the impetus of the Arts and Crafts Movement.

Parallel with this revival was an increasing interest in medieval buildings, which led to a particularly fruitful period of church construction. This interest extended to domestic buildings and large country houses, and led to such remarkable achievements as the (unfinished) Woodchester Mansion near Stroud. This great house, rich in its use of medieval vaulting and buttresses, is a unique mixture of French neo-Gothic theory and Cotswold detailing. The architect, Benjamin Bucknall (1833–95), also designed and adapted cottages for the Woodchester Park estate.

Traditional Cotswold architecture inspired some architects to move to the area and practise the local crafts. Ernest Gimson from Leicestershire, with the Barnsley brothers from Birmingham, moved first to Ewen near Cirencester and then to Pinbury Park, a large house near Sapperton. This they repaired for its owner, Lord Bathurst, but they also extended it with a small rear wing – their first attempt at copying traditional Cotswold construction. As with all buildings of this date, the hand and eye of the architect and designer resulted in a very personal final product which, on close inspection, could not be passed off as a genuine product of the seventeenth century. The chimney was rubble-built (something that the Cotswold craftsman would not do), and there was a distinctive ventilation slit in the gable, unauthentic, but which has none the less been widely copied in modern homes. Internally, a panelled room was

Designed by Benjamin Bucknall, the architect of Woodchester Mansion, this cottage in Nympsfield is inspired by medieval styles. The stone guttering on shaped brackets was recently restored.

constructed, of which the finest aspect is the decorative plasterwork and chimney stone carving, mostly by Gimson.

The Gimson and Barnsley team then moved to cottages which they had built to their own designs in Sapperton; the one that now best illustrates the character and quality of their work is Upper Dorval House. Originally small cottages, they were extended in 1903 by Ernest Barnsley, the only professional architect of the trio. The tower-like addition to the lower end is clearly inspired by the 'High Building' at nearby Daneway House, a building they were loaned for use as showrooms for their furniture.

In the north Cotswolds a larger group, the Guild of Handicrafts, was brought from the east end of London to Chipping Campden in 1902 by C.R. Ashbee, another socialist designer. The group converted the former silk mill to workshops for a wide variety of traditional crafts. Their influence on buildings was more restricted than that of the Sapperton group, although Ashbee was personally responsible for the repair of several Campden houses, among them the Woolstaplers' Hall. This was his first house there, and has since become a museum.

Ashbee's architectural work was not distinctively Cotswold, despite his interest in traditional forms. His own design work, particularly his silverware, was more art nouveau than Arts and Crafts. Perhaps his oddest building was a cottage called The High House in Sheep Street, Chipping Campden, where he extended a traditional cottage upwards and added a gabled roof. The

Upper Dorval House in Sapperton was originally a pair of cottages built around 1800. They were extended in 1903 by Ernest Barnsley, the tower-like addition to the left mimicking the 'High Building' at nearby Daneway, while the lower gabled extension to the right evokes a Cotswold cottage.

original cottage windows were retained on the ground floor, and he used timber casements for all the new windows.

A more major revival of the appreciation of Cotswold architecture was engendered by two books, both published in 1905. The first was part of a national series, *Highways and Byways in . . .*, and the Oxford and the Cotswolds volume, with text by H.A. Evans, was illustrated by Frederick Griggs, a gifted engraver whose work captured much of the simple character and medieval mystery of old buildings. With Norman Jewson – a later addition to the Sapperton group – Griggs formed the Chipping Campden Trust, to repair many of Campden's finest buildings. The other book was *Old Cottages, Farm-Houses and other Stone Buildings in the Cotswold District*, by E. Guy Dawber (later Sir Guy) and the photographer W. Galsworthy Davie. Both Dawber's text and the valuable collection of turn-of-the-century collotype photographs provided further inspiration for several architects who moved to the Cotswolds, especially after the First World War when the area became a popular retirement destination.

The architect and designer C.R. Ashbee's addition of two upper floors to this small cottage in Sheep Street, Chipping Campden, in 1902–3 produced a somewhat quirky result, dominated by the large gable. He retained the original casement windows on the ground floor, and used simple small-paned timber casements above.

This new enthusiasm for a rediscovered Cotswolds led to Broadway becoming a fashionable resort for artists, and eventually for tourists, especially after the Second World War. While the revival of interest in Cotswold architecture did not exactly cause the boom in tourism, it was certainly a contributory factor. Broadway's popularity was soon shared by Bourton-on-the-Water, which has suffered from excessive tourism in the last twenty years.

Chapter 4

NEW LIFE FOR OLD BUILDINGS: CONSERVATION AND ADAPTATION

Living in an old building is of course a very different matter from simply visiting it: old houses have very individual characters, demands and problems, and it is not unheard-of for people to move out of an exquisitely picturesque Cotswold cottage with a sigh of relief rather than of regret, complaining of 'cottage fatigue'. The demands on time and money in daily life do not seem to combine with the particular knowledge and skills needed for building conservation. It is all too tempting to do things the cheap and easy way.

The Cotswolds have a very rich heritage of buildings, but even an understanding of their history and construction methods does not automatically ensure their survival. Building conservation is part technology, part artistic judgement. Balances are sought between what can be adapted and what should be preserved. In an ideal world, all our historic buildings would be retained, fulfilling their historic uses. However, except in perhaps the few cases where buildings are owned by such organizations as the National Trust, this approach is impractical in the present age with its aggressively commercial lifestyle.

Somehow a balance has to be struck between the need to preserve the character of our historic buildings, towns and villages, and allowing them to function as an integral part of a very different modern world. It is true that some buildings will be retained as 'monuments' to their period, but this cannot be expected to occur on a wide scale. A building is not likely to be repaired if it lacks a use, and the best way today of ensuring survival is by allowing sensitive adaptation for modern living. This need not be at the

Individually plain cottages become picturesque by their grouping, such as this row in Bibury. Historic features such as the natural stone roofs and the metal casement windows have survived.

expense of the building's appearance or historic character as long as additions, where required, are well-proportioned and do not interfere with the original building to an unacceptable degree, or result in the removal of original fittings.

So there is very rarely a sound reason why a historic building cannot be fitted out with modern necessities, provided that the designer is suitably inspired, and the owner willing to compromise. Often, the many problems posed in the conversion or adaptation of a historic building lead to architectural solutions of great interest in themselves. Many very successful adaptations are truly inspirational, and this chapter describes a variety of approaches that have been successfully adopted on different Cotswold stone homes.

The choice of a professional to guide the owner of a historic building is crucial. Whether to use an architect, a chartered surveyor, or some other professional designer, will depend very much on the scope of the work. Another issue confronting the owners, or potential owners, of many historic buildings is the range of complex (and often apparently contradictory) rules and regulations imposed by various government bodies. It is tempting to muse on the uncomplicated existence of the original builders of Cotswold stone homes, and on the way in which their freedom to build just as they liked has now been replaced by a world full of laws designed to protect the many idiosyncrasies of these buildings. It may well be the case that employing a professional is essential to obtain all the necessary permissions; at the very least, it provides someone to blame if anything goes wrong.

What is Building Conservation?

It was probably in the Renaissance that Europeans first identified buildings from a past civilization which they thought worthy of emulation, if not preservation. Strewn around the centre of Rome, and scattered over the vast area of its empire, the broken remains of noble monuments began to inspire architects and artists to create a new and modern version of that world. But before they could build, the historic ruins needed to be recorded so that their proportions, details, and construction methods might be copied and adapted. Before long, this new interest in the remains of old buildings led to a desire to see them preserved. It was felt, correctly, that the new age needed such relics, if the sources of inspiration for architects and builders were not to be lost forever.

Throughout the western world today a general agreement has been reached upon the cultural value of historic buildings. This has led to powerful preservation movements, ranging in scale from local civic societies and preservation trusts, through national bodies such as the National Trust and English Heritage, to international organizations such as the International Centre for the Study of the Preservation and the Restoration of Cultural Property (ICCROM), the International Council on Monuments and Sites (ICOMOS), and specialist branches of the United Nations. In the Cotswolds – an area of England which most authorities agree is particularly special – this understanding has produced demands: first, for the protection of buildings by law; and secondly, for craftsmen and designers willing to work in such a constrained context. The aim is to ensure that the historic built environment is not lost, but given a new lease of life so that it will survive and be appreciated by generations to come.

Building conservation is all about ensuring this survival. Perhaps the best-known philosophy of historic building conservation was written by William

Opposite
The village of Whittington with its simple eighteenth-century cottages is currently undergoing a major repair programme. On this cottage there is a mixture of windows – two iron casements in timber sub-frames on the upper floor, a timber casement on the left of the doorway, and a stone-mullioned window on the right.

Lacking picturesque gables or mullioned windows, this plainer type of building (at Bisley) represents the majority of Cotswold houses in its simple, long rectangular plan, and mix of iron-framed, leaded metal casements and sash windows.

Morris in 1877, as a manifesto for a new society, The Society for the Protection of Ancient Buildings. This was primarily aimed at the Victorian restorers, who often removed all traces of the slow evolution of a historic building and substituted their own ideas of how it might perhaps have appeared, in some idealized medieval world. Today, as a result, we are much more concerned to preserve buildings 'warts and all', and to a certain extent to encourage designers to make additions in such a way as to leave the original form of the building clearly discernible to generations to come.

Morris summarized this view in a speech to an annual meeting of the Society, where he concluded that 'these old buildings do not belong to us only; . . . they have belonged to our forefathers and they will belong to our descendants unless we play them false. They are not in any sense our property, to do as we like with. We are only trustees for those who come after us.'

Other societies have since been formed, all looking at building conservation from different points of view, but all broadly following Morris's influential statements. Many are specifically aimed to encourage traditional craftsmanship, while others specialize in the study of different types and periods of buildings. Certain organizations, through their expertise, have acquired a legal consultative role, especially where listed buildings are concerned. (Addresses and descriptions of most of these are listed in Appendix 2.)

While most Cotswold homes were purposely built as dwellings, an increasing number are now the result of conversion from former farm buildings. Traditional farmsteads are falling out of use and, if they are to survive at all, they must be adapted to fulfil a modern need. But Cotswold farm buildings – particularly the imposing blank-walled barns – are very much a feature of the landscape, and too often, no matter how skilful the adaptation, they become rather ill-proportioned houses with gentrified gardens, losing all their sleeping-beauty mystery. The rate at which barns are becoming houses is quite alarming. It may be that soon no one will know what a barn was, or what it was for. The best barns must therefore be preserved without adaptation; but, realistically, many others will either fall down, or be converted to another use.

Two of the case studies below show examples of how farm buildings can be sensitively altered to modern homes, retaining much of their original character. The general approach to building conservation described above equally applies to this more specialized process, although in these cases the role of the designer is crucial.

Today, building conservation in the Cotswolds is concentrated in two areas of interest: first, in ensuring that the modernization of cottages and houses is carried out with the greatest care possible; and secondly, in finding solutions, often of great ingenuity, whereby most of the surplus buildings abandoned by a declining rural culture can be brought into a modern and meaningful use. In both cases the skills required are a combination of traditional craftsmanship and thoughtful design ability, informed by a sound knowledge of the history of traditional architecture.

How to Conserve a Cotswold Stone Home

Where the ardent building conservationist does not yet own a Cotswold stone home, an appropriate building must first be found. Increasingly, estate agents are keeping lists of historic cottages awaiting owners wanting to rescue them from the ravages of time or from the insensitivity of previous occupants. Alternatively, lists of 'Buildings at Risk' are now being prepared by local

The exposed medieval roof in this wing of one of the major houses in Withington is an indication that even the best buildings are still vulnerable and need conservation.

authorities, and it may be a good idea to ask the relevant local council's Conservation Officer whether such a list is available, or whether he or she knows of anything suitable.

If part or all of the building has been unoccupied for a considerable length of time, much work may have to be done. It is often in this first phase, however, that mistakes are made which lead to the removal of significant features. It is rarely necessary to gut a building. Why remove all the old elm or oak floor boards, or take down partitions, when they can be cleaned up and repaired? These may be the very features that make a building feel old, with all their irregularities and signs of wear and tear.

Specialist advisors may well be required from the beginning of the project. Their calm expertise will help to cushion the shock of some of the horrors that may lie in wait. Lists of architects and surveyors may be obtained from their relevant national institutes, while building and craft organizations also keep lists of members. (The addresses of these organizations are in Appendix 2.) Perhaps the worst problem is dry rot. This is a fungus that grows in moist, unventilated conditions, usually – although not exclusively – on wood. Once it takes hold, it can spread through plaster and even masonry. It feeds on the wood, reducing it to a crumbling pile of dust, and so is scarcely desirable in the main structural timbers. Some expert companies today are able to destroy the rot without removing very much timber. This is particularly important if the affected timber includes the original moulded beams, or panelling.

Dampness in walls and floors is another common defect. Historically, stone cottages were kept dry by having large fires burning almost constantly, driving the moisture to the outside part of the wall. Such fuel consumption today is not acceptable, either from the economic or the environmental point of view. Ventilation such as that provided by cracks between floorboards or under doors is now no longer acceptable. The Building Regulations (which generally apply to new construction) impose very high insulation and damp-proofing requirements, although it is not always possible to introduce these standards into an old building without being unacceptably destructive. Where floors are made of stone, the slabs should be carefully lifted and stored while a new damp-proof membrane is laid. The flags can then be re-set, although some may disintegrate during this process and require replacement.

The damp-proofing of walls is a little more difficult, as the most common (rubble) construction is somewhat unpredictable and inconsistent in composition. Injected chemical damp-proof courses sometimes work, although often these cannot span the whole thickness of the wall. Rising damp may not be totally eliminated, despite the manufacturer's promises. Alternatively, a damp-proofing treatment can be applied to the inside face of

Many Cotswold cottages are built into hillsides, such as here at Duntisbourne Abbots, resulting in damp problems. Sometimes, however, a narrow trench was originally dug beside the wall, which has become filled in and overgrown, but is well worth restoring.

the wall, especially if it is below ground level. Again, a frequent result is simply to drive the dampness further up the wall, to emerge at a higher and often much more visible level. Modern external treatments, especially silicones, should always be avoided on stone buildings. It is clear that there can be few guarantees of success in dealing with damp problems in stone buildings. Often the best approach is to test one or two of the more reversible treatments in small areas, and judge their effectiveness. Attention must always be paid to the need for the building to 'breathe', something often ill-understood and too rarely considered.

Most of this work will only be undertaken once the overall plan for the adaptation of the building has been settled. It is at this stage that a professional advisor will almost certainly be required, and it is preferable that the same person should draw the plans for any permissions that may be required, and also produce the more detailed specifications and schedules necessary for prices to be obtained from builders.

Whether an architect is employed, or a chartered surveyor, is often not very important. Whoever is selected should be experienced in dealing with old buildings; and if the building has any special restrictions (such as being listed, or situated in a conservation area) the advisor should be experienced in taking owners through the complex web of legislation surrounding such restrictions and making the necessary applications for permission. It is a good idea to ask to see other buildings successfully repaired or adapted by the professional concerned. Some advice may be given by the local council; they will usually avoid making any specific recommendations, but may have lists of architects, surveyors, builders or specialist craftsmen in the area.

Once he or she is appointed, the owner will be very much in the hands of the advisor, although it is important that the designs take the owner's special needs into account. Often the best adaptations are those that embrace a few eccentricities resulting from the peculiar circumstances of the building and the type of accommodation required. In the case of converted farm buildings, the most successful examples are those very much tailor-made for their owner's tastes. Generalized – perhaps purely speculative – conversions are commonly bland and lacking in sensitivity: by trying to please everyone, the designer is pleasing no one.

Another pitfall which may occur is to find that the appointed architect undertakes no personal involvement in your project beyond the writing of covering letters for his fee account: the actual work is done by a rather brash and partly qualified student. In the best architectural practices dealing with old buildings, the person appointed is the one who sees the job through to the end (although it is unrealistic to expect him or her to produce all the drawings).

Opposite
Cottages like John Brown's Cottage at Ablington near Bibury should be preserved as small buildings, with any extensions kept to a minimum. All too often such cottages are engulfed in large new additions, resulting in 'mini-manor houses'.

Another professional who may need to be involved if the building is in a particularly poor condition is a structural engineer. Again, selection of the right person is important. If you have already appointed an architect or surveyor, it is usually best to take their advice on whom to employ. Some structural engineers are particularly skilled in dealing with historic buildings, and understand the usual slight shifts in masonry that are to be expected in walls over two hundred years old. Others, however, will believe every unevenness is something to eradicate, and will not be happy until they have rebuilt most of the masonry. Such an approach is destructive, expensive, and no substitute for repairing the historic structure as it stands. In addition, such an over-zealous approach will almost certainly remove all traces of the building's history, producing something that resembles the original house, but is, in fact, nothing more than a replica.

Good structural engineers will be slow to suggest radical repairs, except in the direst of emergencies. Usually, the first step will be to check on the building's movement. It should be remembered that all old buildings move to a certain extent, the structure expanding and contracting through the seasons but usually returning to its original position over a full year. This 'breathing' is normal, and should never be prevented by the insertion of rigid modern structural elements such as reinforced concrete or steel. Non-flexible modern structures can often cause further, more serious, problems or even unexpectedly promote partial collapse. An engineer who does not understand these issues (which require appreciably different techniques from those used on modern buildings) should not be working on historic structures.

One of the commonest problems with rubble stonework is a loss of strength in a wall due to the washing-out of mortar and of the loose rubble in the middle of the wall. This is a particular problem if the building has lost its roof, and is the reason why such buildings should have their wall tops protected as a matter of some urgency. The use of cement-based grouts injected into the wall once the pointing has been made good has been the usual solution to this problem, although lime-and-ash mixes are now preferred, a material which more closely resembles the original fill in strength and porosity.

Many Cotswold buildings are fortunate in being built on a hard rock base, very close to the ground surface. There are many others, however, that are built with no foundations at all; or which, if built on clay, may have settled into a twisted shape over the years. The job of the structural engineer in this instance is to ensure that any major settlement of the masonry has stopped, and to try to alleviate stresses caused by the changed wall positions. In extreme cases a concrete foundation may have to be constructed beneath the existing walls by a process called underpinning, but this should be possible without any demolition.

Changes in internal room arrangements, and particularly the insertion of new timber staircases, often damage the building's stability by cutting through beams and floor joists. This is important because the upper floor structures also tie together the opposite walls, and the loss of this reinforcement allows the walls to bow outwards. It is very common to see a bulge half-way up the walls of a Cotswold building, resulting from some past alteration. Bulging walls can be supported from the exterior by buttresses, and historically this was the way many Cotswold houses were repaired, giving them the somewhat medieval appearance which was itself thought desirable in the Victorian era. Alternatively, internal iron (or, in modern times, steel) tie bars may have been or can be fitted, with a variety of patterns of ironwork used on the outer face of the wall to spread the pulling force.

In all cases, it is vital that the owner seeks guidance with structural work, even where the majority of the work is being carried out on a do-it-yourself basis. A good source of guidance can be the local council's Building Control Officer, who normally deals with the law covering building construction standards. While old buildings are not normally expected to comply with the standards laid down in these regulations, any new work, such as extensions, normally must do so. If a professional advisor is used, he or she should deal with issues relating to the Building Regulations; alternatively, your builder can attend to this.

Apart from the walls, the other main element of the building is the roof, traditionally covered with Cotswold stone slates. Where the building is listed, it is usual for the local council's Conservation Officer to insist on the retention of the original stone – although if this has decayed very badly new stone slates may be required. Until recently, stone slate production was at such a low level as to be able to provide slates only for repairs to the most important Cotswold buildings. Luckily there has been a revival in stone slate production, and there are now three active quarries in the Cotswold area (see Appendix 2). Prices are still high, but it is rare for a whole roof to require replacement. Usually about half the old stone slates should be salvageable, so these are normally concentrated on the front slopes, while the new, initially looking a little brash in colour, are used at the back.

The cost of a major re-roofing operation is perhaps one of the greatest burdens for the owner of a Cotswold house. It is very sad that in Great Britain (unlike other countries) no special support is available from the government to assist in this work, and even the tax system provides no means of discounting the cost. Time after time a major 'crunch' is reached when an owner, particularly of a listed building, is caught between the need to keep the stone roof, and the scale of the costs involved. This burden is particularly heavy for surviving estates owning a large number of stone-roofed cottages and farm buildings.

Stone slate may be specified in repairs or alterations to a listed building. Sadly, there are now very few local suppliers or traditional slaters.

If this treasure of stone roofs is to survive, and the crafts of quarrying and making the stone slates are to continue, it is clear that some concessions should be made – perhaps by the removal of VAT from the cost of the operation, for example. The Cotswolds, together with other areas of the country where traditional materials and repair techniques are expensive, are poorly served in this important respect.

Imitation stone roofing slates have been produced for some time now, but because of the casting process used to produce them, they never have the infinite variety of size and texture of natural stone slates, and rarely have a realistic colour. It is true that in recent years one or two manufacturers have produced a more expensive, and somewhat more realistic, product. But it also seems that the more effort put into making increasingly accurate imitations, the higher the production costs. Perhaps one day the perfect imitation will be produced – costing more than a quarried and hand-dressed stone slate!

Windows and doors form another very important, but less financially crippling, part of the building for consideration. Iron casement windows in stone-mullioned openings deserve great care. If possible, they should be repaired by a blacksmith, and increasingly this skill is being revived. Modern metal casements – although an improvement from the damp and draught-proofing point of view – are not the same in their detailing, and they should not be installed as replacements unless it is absolutely certain that the original iron casements are beyond repair.

If replacement is necessary, two parts of the original window should be salvaged. First, the glass: if it is at all old, it is of as much historic interest as the window frame. The small panes should be very carefully removed, and the window-maker should be asked to use these in the new window, if necessary making up the quantity with thin horticultural glass, which has similar imperfections to old glass.

Secondly, the old casement fasteners and stay-bars should be taken off the old window frame and re-used. These are often simple in design, but far superior to any off-the-peg product of today. Sometimes some of the older fittings may have already been lost, but again, local craftsmen should be able to produce copies to make up numbers.

In this cottage at Duntisbourne Leer, the leaded iron casement is in a timber frame and under a timber lintel. The pigeon holes above suggest that it was originally built as a stable or other outbuilding.

Great care should also be taken with the timber windows (whether with iron-framed casements or not) commonly used in the eighteenth and nineteenth centuries. The most common defect is rotting of the cill and bottom frame of the opening casement. A good local joiner can replace these components at a fraction of the cost of a complete new window, saving a historic feature as well as the owner's money. Sash windows rarely require complete replacement and again, a good local craftsman can carry out the necessary repairs relatively cheaply, copying the original mouldings and glazing bars precisely.

Historic doors, whether panelled or of simple boarded construction, should always be repaired and retained. Their detailing provides essential evidence as to when the building was built or altered. A common tendency today is to strip panelled doors, particularly pine. These were always intended to be painted, pine being the lowest quality of timber, often knotty and marked. Good traditional paint colours and types of paint are now available in certain manufacturers' ranges.

Converting Farm Buildings

Despite much legitimate concern, the conversion of redundant farm buildings to dwellings is a reality which must be faced. It represents one of the greatest challenges to modern ideas of conservation, as obviously the functions for which farm buildings were constructed in the past were quite different from those of modern dwelling-houses.

Barns were simply large sheds, with porches extended out at mid-points to help shelter the harvest waggons waiting to be unloaded, and with a timber-floored 'midstrey' area used as a threshing floor for the crops. Later adaptations were made by the introduction of lofts at each end, allowing high-level access to the steam-powered threshing machines introduced in the nineteenth century. The crops were thrown up into these lofts through pitching holes, with shuttered openings introduced usually (although not exclusively) in the gable ends.

Some of the grandest and oldest barns were built on monastic estates, and were designed to store one-tenth – the 'tithe' – of the tenant farmers' production for direct use by the monastery. Pigeons were also kept in barns, many of which incorporate dovecotes in their gable ends, or in specially constructed gabled lofts over the porches. Pigeons were the preserve of manors or monasteries and of those associated with them, as a source of fresh eggs, meat, and droppings for fertilizer.

Field barns were built where the land controlled by a farm was too extensive for crops and cattle to be brought back to the farmstead on a daily

basis. These barns usually have attached shelter-sheds for cattle, together with other elaborations such as calving pens and stables. Field barns exist on the largest, and often last, farms to be created by enclosure of the open wolds, up to the early nineteenth century. Other farm buildings were designed for different purposes, such as cart sheds, stables for farm horses, and granaries for storing grain.

Abandoned, with its stone slate roof long since replaced with corrugated iron, this barn near Guiting Power has received planning permission for conversion to a house. Widespread conversions have resulted in untouched barns becoming an endangered species.

This rich heritage of buildings is now generally redundant. While many farm buildings are of such quality as to require preservation as they stand – possibly through museums of rural life, or through uses that do not need any alteration work – the majority must either be allowed to fall down, or be converted to another, financially viable use.

The most difficult farm buildings to convert sensitively are barns. Their large expanses of rubble walling result in an austere character that can easily be lost once windows and doorways are introduced. Two of the case studies are designed to show how, by exercising very careful architectural judgement, this apparently intractable design problem can be solved.

Case Studies

Having examined the philosophy and methods of building conservation, and looked at the process of starting repairs on an old stone building, the next issue to be considered is the design of the adaptation.

Six Cotswold stone homes, either created from original domestic buildings or converted from farm buildings, are described in the remainder of this chapter. The selection covers a broad range of possibilities, and is primarily intended to give practical advice and inspiration to both present and potential Cotswold stone home owners. The examples also illustrate a variety in the scale of building, and the extent of work involved.

CASE STUDY 1: FARMHOUSE REPAIR IN A SOUTH COTSWOLD VALLEY

Towards the south-western end of the Cotswold escarpment, between the towns of Stroud and Dursley, the landscape becomes more dramatic than on the main Cotswold plateau. Steep-sided valleys are topped by beech woods and drained by fast-running rivers. Into this landscape grew the woollen

The rather bleak and uncared-for look of the south Cotswold farmhouse, before work started.

industry, and one of its lesser-known centres is the small valley of the River Ewelme. Branching off this are a number of side combes, and in one of these is a previously somewhat neglected farmhouse.

The main building faces east, with a garden as a forecourt. As with so many farmhouses, the building has accumulated over different periods, the main part being about two hundred years old. Behind this is an earlier structure, more modest in scale and now almost engulfed in the later building. It may have been built in the seventeenth century but is now (after many periodic alterations) very difficult to identify in detail. The north end of the house, latterly used as a milking parlour, was almost certainly originally part of the house.

The whole farmstead has a quaint, slightly run-down feel, and was seen as a bargain. Its untouched atmosphere, together with its almost magical hill-bound setting, attracted the new owners to buy the house as their family home. The house contains four large bedrooms but lacked a modern kitchen, and the bathrooms needed complete modernization. However, the first essentials were to repair the stonework, and to replace the fairly recently home-made windows on the main frontage.

First, all the masonry was inspected to assess the extent of repair required. As is often the case, substantial areas of perfectly sound lime mortar survived. It was decided that the mortar should only be replaced where it was defective, or

The extent to which this formerly bleak farmhouse façade has been enhanced is shown here after installation of the new sash windows. One old window remains in place, where the owners intend to add an appropiately detailed bay window at a future date.

Purpose-made sash windows are here carefully installed into the original window openings.

in areas where new stonework was to be inserted. Correctly, lime mortars were used. Joints were well raked out to at least 1 in (25 mm) in depth before re-pointing started. The type of pointing was carefully selected to match the 'struck' pointing common in the Cotswolds during the early nineteenth century, a period when the stone was often laid to courses, as on the front elevation here.

The second task was to decide on the likely design of the original windows, and if possible to have replicas made. One common fear with owners is that purpose-made windows will be very expensive, and that it is difficult to find joiners to make them. This is fortunately not the case throughout most of the Cotswold area, as many old-fashioned joinery businesses survive, and many local builders still have their own joinery workshops.

After the existing window openings had been measured and drawn out, various designs were considered. The original windows might have been side-hung casements, but taking into consideration a likely construction date of 1800 or 1820 and the tendency to use more up-to-date designs on garden frontages, a sash window was selected. In order to fit the proportions of the openings, an eight-over-eight pattern common from about 1800 to 1850 was chosen. The panes of glass in such a sash are very small, since only larger and more important houses merited the larger panes which were then in production. All the glazing bars were moulded on the inside, with a rather more elaborate moulding than was common at the time. The meeting rails (the two horizontal frame members that fit one alongside the other when the two halves of the window are closed) were made so that their dimensions, when viewed from the outside, were the same as those of the sides of the sash frames, a refinement which ensures an evenness of depth of frame around the whole window.

The overall result is a much more appropriate and handsome frontage, which is not only visually pleasing but adds to the market value of the property, well beyond the relatively small expenditure involved. It is just such careful consideration of masonry repairs and window restoration that can make a Cotswold stone home rescue scheme a great success.

CASE STUDY 2: MILLER'S HOUSE IN THE STROUD VALLEY

The steep sides of the Stroud valley have produced some interesting permutations of Cotswold architectural style, many houses and cottages being jammed into hillsides on very constricted sites. This former mill owner's house is just such a building, with four storeys at one end and two at the other. In fact, it is possible to enter the attic through a gable-end door off the lane!

Although the building had been neglected, the relative lack of previous modernization meant that there were many historic features for its present

Opposite
The cramped but pleasantly secluded siting of the mill owner's house can be seen in this view of the steeply terraced 'hanging garden'. The original corners of the cottage are marked by dressed stone quoins, and the change of stonework above the pair of mullioned windows indicates that the roof height has been raised, probably to accommodate a weaver's loft.

owners to repair and keep. The first problem was that the original hall, with a very large fireplace, was taken up by a modern kitchen; the fireplace was hidden by modern brickwork and wallpaper. A small and incongruous fire-surround was removed, and the fireplace opened up. Since a kitchen was now needed, a cellar was used for the purpose, reached by a previously forgotten stone staircase. This cellar is now a modern 'galley' kitchen, and using a staircase to reach it seems only a minor inconvenience.

Above the kitchen, lit by a sash window, is a very fine panelled room with a stone fireplace. The owners have carefully repaired both fireplace and panelling, and the proportions of this room can now be appreciated. It illustrates the quality of life that even the lesser mill owners aspired to, even if the room does seem to have been built at about half the correct size.

A spiral staircase, in the characteristic position next to the fireplace, leads to the main upper floor. While all the rooms are small, skilful design has resulted in the convenient location of cupboards and bathrooms. The main bathroom was created in a former bedroom, and is reached through what was once a wall cupboard. The change in level was utilized to allow the bath to appear sunken into the floor, although in fact the floor level has been raised.

Further up the spiral staircase is the attic, with two more bedrooms and a small bathroom. The latter is slightly Edwardian in character (the first age of great bathroom design), while the bedrooms seem almost to float among the roof timbers.

Buried in the depths of walls in even the most modest cottages, large stone fireplaces can remain in place, covered over and long forgotten. Here work has just started and the small modern tiled fireplace has not yet been removed.

During the eighteenth century, this magnificent, although very small, panelled room was fitted into the earlier building. A fashionable sash window was also provided despite the retention of the traditional stone-mullioned windows elsewhere in the building. Preserving this evolution is not only cheaper, but preferred to returning the building to an ideal 'original' condition.

Externally it may appear that little has happened. In fact, a rather ugly brick-built kitchen wing connecting at first-floor level has been demolished, returning the building to something of its former contour-stepping simplicity. Windows have been repaired, and leaded glass reinstated. The latter was undertaken, one window at a time, by simply fitting new glazing into existing metal casements; these were also given convincing seventeenth-century-style fasteners, made by the local blacksmith.

This project, which is still not complete, demonstrates that by doing only a little at a time, particular care can be taken over the work and consequently much more of the character of a building can be preserved. By using the most appropriate modern fittings, and by keeping and re-using existing fittings as much as possible, the cost of the work can be considerably reduced.

The massive stonework around the now-revealed hall fireplace quite dwarfs the furniture. To the left – just visible – are the stone spiral stairs, here in their usual position next to the fireplace, built into the thicker wall at this point.

It is also noteworthy that this elaborate and intricate adaptation was accomplished without the services of an architect. Although one was initially consulted, the scheme he produced was thought too destructive and expensive to be pursued. Spending large sums on extensive alterations is desirable neither from the conservation nor from the financial viewpoint, and the owners of this house have shown great skill in creating a well-considered, sensitive design.

CASE STUDY 3: VILLAGE COTTAGE BY THE UPPER RIVER WINDRUSH

'Cotswold cottages have mullioned windows, don't they?' This is the usual, and often quite correct, assumption of visitors to the Cotswolds. But by the nineteenth century, timber casements of a fairly standard design were normally installed, requiring some form of arched or lintel support to the stonework above. Timber casements in stone arches became as common as stone-mullioned windows.

Because natural stone-mullioned windows are expensive, modernizing 'improvers' once tended to leave existing timber casements well alone, but the post-war introduction of cast imitation stone seems to have brought mullioned windows within the reach of the average pocket. Unfortunately, the appearance of the cast material is never the same as natural stone, and the castings are not correct enough in their detailing to appear quite right. Many originally timber-windowed cottages have had modern mullioned windows fitted, destroying their own particular history as well as their appearance.

Regrettably, the cost of reinstating the correct windows is usually prohibitive – but it did not deter the new owner of this idyllic cottage by the upper reaches of the River Windrush. On the contrary, he was enthusiastic to do everything possible to return the building to its original glory.

Perhaps the casual observer, looking at the cottage from the village street (which runs right past the end gable, after crossing the stone bridge), would fail to appreciate the extent of work involved. All now looks calm and tranquil, with perhaps only the newly pointed walls indicating that any

Situated by a stone bridge over the River Windrush, the cottage has once again become typical of the simple casement-windowed cottages so common in the mid-Cotswolds.

The restored original window openings of the cottage may be seen here with the repaired cider-mill house at the end of the cottage, on which stone slates now replace the corrugated iron.

changes have been made. All good conservation is like this: it often seems as if nothing has happened to the building since its original construction.

But in fact, all the white-painted timber windows in their stone arches are new; before, they were all off-the-peg, dull grey, imitation stone-mullioned casements with meanly detailed hood-moulds. The frontage once looked gaunt and uninviting; now, it is hard to resist going into the garden to see it better. A further successful detail is to be found at the far end of the cottage.

What was once apparently no more than a small, rather unprepossessing iron-roofed shed was discovered to contain one of the wonders of the village: an intact cider mill, together with a dismantled press.

The present owner has incorporated the cider mill into a sensitive adaptation of the shed, which is now used as the kitchen, dominated by the huge stone wheel and circular mill trough. While living 'around the mill' may seem an unlikely solution, the owner has preserved something of value for future generations. Such imagination follows William Morris's idea that present occupants are trustees for those who come after them. It would not be impossible, in the future, for someone to remove the kitchen fittings and the glazed screens, return the mill to working order, harness a horse to it, and start making cider in the traditional Cotswold way. It might even encourage a revival of the traditional apple varieties – but that's another story!

CASE STUDY 4: SMALL COTTAGE IN THE UPPER FROME VALLEY

Many smaller cottages are to be found in the south-western part of the Cotswolds, linked to the former woollen industry of that area. They are often of one or two rooms per floor with a lean-to extension added later to provide a scullery. As described in the previous chapter, cooking in these very small buildings took place in a general-purpose hall, and until recently the only

Cottages in the upper Frome valley are typically as simple as this one, photographed before work started.

155

concession to twentieth-century living has been the refitting of the scullery to provide a kitchen and downstairs bathroom.

This is just such a cottage. Its origins must be linked to weaving, as it is built to exactly the same pattern as the many small weavers' cottages in Stroud valley villages such as Eastcombe, Bussage and Chalford Hill. The plan is typical, with the scullery lean-to extension to the rear, and two first-floor bedrooms, one leading into the other. It still has its original spiral staircase, in the usual position next to the main fireplace. But who now would put up with a small bathroom partitioned off from the generously-sized (if ill-appointed) kitchen? The latter had a stone sink in one corner and a lonely sit-up-and-beg cooker in the other: not exactly a cosy and inviting 'heart' of the house.

The character of such cottages is particularly fragile. All too often they are expanded into mini-manor houses, losing all trace of their humble, industrial

The new extension was designed to fit behind the front of the cottage, and replace the existing rear extension.

Tucked behind the main part of the cottage these weatherstones, designed to protect the junction between the wall and lower roof, could easily be forgotten, but were carefully preserved during the building work.

origins. How to improve the accommodation to tolerable modern standards while not spoiling the building's character was the problem facing the owner.

The original part of the cottage is a simple rectangle in plan, set well back from the village street. The later scullery lean-to sits behind, and largely out of sight. Either the cottage could acquire a new wing, leaving the scullery untouched; or the extension could be tucked behind the old cottage, replacing the scullery and leaving little change in the appearance of the building as seen from the road. As the lean-to scullery was of little architectural interest, the latter solution was adopted. What the owner needed was a bathroom on the first floor, and a more conventional layout of bedrooms with separate entrances. The stone spiral stair was retained, as there was no room for a large new staircase – a sound decision, in any case, from the preservation point of view. The extension was designed to sit directly to the rear of the cottage, and to avoid disproportion it was given two small gables, one set back from the other.

One of the most interesting features, at the back of the cottage, is a series of stepped weather-stones, the traditional means of protecting a lower roof slope abutting a stone wall; these were preserved by a careful alignment of the extension roof, which also allowed the retention of a stone chimney, giving a modestly picturesque quality to the side view.

Another consideration was the treatment of the new stone for the extension. Unless old stone is used (and this nearly always requires the demolition of another Cotswold building – something not to be encouraged), new walls will look bright and perhaps a little harsh in colour. Presumably, all Cotswold buildings looked bright when they were newly built, so this should not be of particular concern. In the south Cotswolds, however, and particularly in the Frome Valley, the rubble-built cottages were originally limewashed, usually in ochre or cream shades, but sometimes in a bright white. Therefore, to help 'tone down' the new stone, and as a historically appropriate finish, the owner decided to apply a coating of limewash. Ironically, this has given rise to expressions of surprise, and some ill-informed opposition from neighbours. The owner is therefore delaying this final stage until public relations are eased. It is to be hoped that an increased knowledge of the use of limewash and its practical benefits will allay such fears – especially in areas such as this, where limewashing cottage walls must once have been as natural an activity as washing the car at weekends is now.

A further improvement carried out in the course of building operations was the replacement of the modern concrete-tiled front roof of the cottage with a new natural stone roof, while one of the better types of imitation stone slates was used on the new extension roof at the rear.

Shown in the middle of the project, the original chimney of the old rear wing is carefully preserved while work proceeds around it. The very noticeable joints in the new stonework (bottom right) will become less obvious once pointing is carried out.

The successful way in which the character of this small cottage has been preserved can be seen here. The extensions are barely visible, while the new stone slate roof at the front is a major improvement.

Preserving the character of even the smallest cottage is possible if great care is taken in the design of any extension. Any interesting historical features can be preserved in their original positions. The result is a home suitable for at least the next hundred years, but still clearly the product of the great late seventeenth-century boom in cottage building.

CASE STUDY 5: COACH HOUSE IN THE NORTH COTSWOLDS

Coach houses, particularly this rather grand one next to a north Cotswold manor house, have an advantage over barns as far as conversion is concerned in that they at least have openings on the ground floor, and already have an upper floor. Their exterior is often more domestic in appearance than that of barns, so to some extent the problems of conversion are limited to the treatment of the coach arches, the fitting-out of the interior, and (perhaps most importantly) the method of getting light into the upper floor.

In this case the arched frontage of the coach house is clearly visible from the main village road. The open situation of the building made it difficult to select parts of the external wall where new window and door openings might easily be concealed from view. Great care was especially required as the coach

The row of five coach arches dominates the north elevation of the coach house, before work started. (Photograph: Toby Falconer.)

house forms part of one of the most picturesque groups of buildings in the northern Cotswolds, the manor house being of particular interest while the small adjoining church is Norman in date.

Glazed screens in the barn doorways are one of the most obvious indications that 'conversion' has taken place, and the huge areas of glass often look quite forbidding. Since it was going to be obvious that the building was a conversion of a coach house, it was determined that high-quality joinery should be the key feature of the design. The architect decided on a fairly traditional approach, glazing above a waist-high rail and dividing the opening into evenly-sized panels. Two related screen types were designed, one with more glazing than the other, and were alternated along the five arches.

An even more fundamental decision was the treatment of the joinery. All too often a variety of timber stain is used which ranges from a near-violet 'mahogany' to a vibrant, almost orange, shade of ginger. There is no reason why such unlikely colours should be selected. The joinery of unconverted farm buildings shows that most was either untreated and left to silver with age, or was tarred. The resulting colours were a grey or a near-black – both colours which are now available in serveral manufacturers' stain ranges, so there is no excuse for not producing quite effective imitations of this traditional appearance. The joinery on many estate farm buildings was

Inside the coach house, the beams and joists are all visible, as are the arches before the carefully designed timber screens were installed. (Photograph: Toby Falconer.)

painted, especially when they were situated in villages, so paint is quite acceptable as a finish, although it seems to be less popular at present. In this building a grey-green paint was selected which does not attract unnecessary attention to the infilled arches; and the building, at first glance, looks very much a part of the farm group.

The other main problem was how to get light into the former granary, which, before conversion, was lit only by small windows at either end. Roof-lights have been used extensively and indiscriminately in the past, but as they set glass at a very reflective angle, and require complicated flashing arrangements to make them waterproof, they usually break up the roofscape to an unacceptable extent.

Traditional dormer windows were used here, relating the coach house to the adjacent manor house, which has several dormers in the stone roof. Great care was taken to ensure that the detailing matched that on the house. This averted such common mistakes as over-wide cheeks (the sides of the dormer), and vertical fascias fixed to the cheeks. The dormers (three on the front elevation, well spread out, and one at the rear) were hipped to match the house, although on farm buildings gabled dormers would normally be much more common.

The rear of the coach house was completely blank, but somehow a front and back door had to be accommodated, as this was the direction from which

In this case, the dormer windows and screens in the arched entrances seem hardly to have disturbed the original appearance of the coach house. Even the chimney seems quite in character.

the building was to be approached. It would have been all too easy to create a domestic-looking door arrangement, destroying the characteristic 'blank' character of the back of the building. In the end, the main doorway was positioned under the central rear dormer window and the 'back' door was set at one end. This left large areas of blank wall intact.

With its simple treatment of the arches, sensible use of traditional dormer windows, and careful design of door openings, the exterior of the coach house is a credit to the close collaboration between architect and owner that is surely one of the most important keys to success. A final touch was to match the nineteenth-century 'struck' pointing, an often-neglected aspect of stone building repair. While the replacement pointing looks a little new, it will soon tone down and be noticeable only on the very closest inspection.

CASE STUDY 6: BARN CONVERSION IN THE SOUTH-EAST COTSWOLDS

At the extreme south-eastern corner of the Cotswolds, near the Thames-side towns of Fairford and Lechlade, the landscape flattens out and villages are no longer tucked below valley contours. This area was the last in the Cotswolds to be enclosed for farming, mostly around the beginning of the nineteenth century. It was a period of barn-building on a larger scale than before, and it is in this area that many of the finest Cotswold barns are to be found.

Just such a grand barn is this, rubble-built with a slightly off-centre threshing floor, and a gabled porch on one side only. A pigeon loft, with the timber cupola breaking the roof-line, makes the barn highly picturesque. The walls have rather distinctive triangular air-vents, simply made with three large slabs of stone. Attached to one end of the barn is a stable wing, somewhat altered by previous owners.

The present owner wanted to provide an annexe to the nearby farmhouse, but it was considered particularly important to keep the plain character of the barn exterior and as much as possible of the lofty timber interior. Fortunately, as is often the case, the attached stable allowed for one bedroom, the kitchen and a bathroom to be outside the barn space, so that the only rooms to be partitioned off the main interior void were a galleried bedroom and a quiet study over the porch. The area beneath the bedroom gallery was put to use for dining, while the main barn space became a lofty living room, with a stove at the far end.

Light was allowed into the barn simply by glazing the barn doorways, but to avoid the usual gaunt effect the doors themselves were retained, and can be shut, making the building look like a barn again. A more difficult task was letting light into the bedroom gallery. The choice appeared to be between dormer windows and roof-lights. The former have the great disadvantage of breaking up a simple roof form, while the latter introduce reflective panels of glass, drawing attention to the fact that the building is no longer used as a barn. The final choice seems obvious in retrospect, but is often forgotten by designers trying to grapple with barn conversions: to install some windows just below the roof eaves. These five windows were designed to be as simple and un-domestic as possible, being square in shape and fairly small so as not to detract much from the effect of plain walling. They rather suggest pigeon-holes for oversized pigeons! The effect is distinctly rural, rather than domestic.

The new window joinery was all very simple in detail. No attempt was made even to suggest that the barn was domestic. The result is somewhat utilitarian, but none the less elegant in its functional directness. Any

The simple lines of the barn are shown, before building work started.

suggestion of bleakness has been avoided by the addition of a lean-to roofed terrace on the less interesting (and reasonably obscured) south elevation.

The main message from this well-judged, inventive and sensitive design is that there are four main points to consider in converting barns to houses. First, the massiveness of the walls must be preserved by very careful

Just how much of the barn's character was preserved can be seen in these before-and-after views of the interior. The roof structure has been left visible and the bedroom gallery has been installed at the far end, while light floods the space from glazed doors in the barn doorway openings. Behind the stainless-steel railings, the loft has become a 'quiet area' for study, reached by a ladder.

positioning of windows and doors, and by avoiding at all costs the use of domestic-looking casements. Secondly, the treatment of the main barn doorways should be very carefully thought through: retain the barn doors, keep the joinery simple, and above all avoid the blank expression seen on the faces of so many former barns today resulting from the use of vast expanses of glass. Thirdly, the roofscape should be kept as clear of visual interruptions as possible. Dormers or roof-lights are equally undesirable in this respect, so – if the roof height allows – fit windows under the eaves, and design them as simply as possible. Finally, preserve as much of the interior barn space as possible, diverting partitioned accommodation into any attached outbuildings.

From these examples it should be clear that there are many ways in which Cotswold buildings can be adapted without any loss of their character. This process has all the potential for being truly creative, adding something of our own age of all the more value because it allows the retention of worthwhile elements from the past. Building conservation at its best is precisely that – an

activity which uniquely seems to bring together the techniques of preservation, and design skills often missing from the bland modern buildings of today. It is no wonder that the public, whether tourists or residents, have voted with their feet and come to the Cotswolds, and if they are to continue to do so, building conservation and the creation of Cotswold stone homes for the future must play their part.

Viewed from the front, little seems to have changed. The building is still clearly a barn, and shows that with skilful design, and willing owners, a very high quality result may be achieved.

CONSERVATION AND BUILDING LEGISLATION

Listed Buildings

The idea of a list of protected historic buildings was put into practice in the Town and Country Planning Act (1947). This provided for a 'List of Buildings of Special Architectural or Historic Interest' to be produced by experts, and for some statutory control and protection to be given to the buildings included on the list. The first lists were then drawn up, and buildings were graded by importance. The best buildings were Grade I; those less interesting but very worthy of preservation, Grade II; while those that should be preserved, but did not actually receive any legal protection, were Grade III.

Today, the current act – the Planning (Listed Buildings and Conservation Areas) Act (1990) – embodies some quite detailed controls. Any works affecting the character of a listed building, whether for complete or partial demolition or dismantling, permanent alteration, certain repairs, or even changes of decorative colour scheme, can result in the need for a formal application to the local council for listed building consent. These controls apply as much to the interior as to the exterior of the building, contrary to a common but misplaced belief that only the exterior of a listed building is protected.

Since 1968 the grading of listed buildings has been revised. The old list of Grade III (and therefore unprotected) buildings was scrapped, and a complete national re-survey of all historic buildings has been carried out. Now the buildings are classified as Grade I, Grade II* (called 'two-star') and Grade II.

The buildings listed at Grades I and II* are regarded as outstanding, so in certain situations they can be subject to grants from English Heritage. About 2 per cent of all listed buildings are Grade I, while about 4 per cent are Grade II*. The vast majority (94 per cent) are Grade II. There are now in total about 450,000 listed buildings in England.

Not only is the building itself protected, but so are any structures attached to it, such as outbuildings, walls or railings, and any buildings within its 'curtilage'. The precise meaning of the latter word has been the subject of intense legal debate, but generally the curtilage would include, for example, the garden of a house, or the farmyard of a farmhouse. Any buildings within that curtilage at the time the building was listed, and used in conjunction with the main listed building, are 'deemed to be listed', and must be treated as if they are on the list themselves. The exception to this is where the curtilage building was built later than 1 July 1948.

If work is carried out to a listed building and no prior permission has been granted, the owner, and the person carrying out the work can, at worst, be liable to a criminal prosecution. Recent cases have resulted in the imposition of very significant fines on the owners of listed buildings who sought to demolish them without permission.

It is therefore advisable always to speak to the local council's Conservation Officer before preparing detailed plans for work to a listed building, as generally they will be only too pleased to provide free expert advice on an informal basis. Those thinking of buying a listed building should also follow this suggestion, especially if any changes to the building are under consideration.

Another consequence of the listing of a building is the power it confers on the local council if action to preserve the building is needed. Urgent works notices can be served requiring temporary protective work or propping to be carried out by the owner, and these give the council power to carry out the work itself and reclaim the cost of this from the owner if nothing is done within the period of time stipulated on the order. In major cases, where temporary works would be insufficient, a full repairs notice can be served, which requires owners to restore a listed building completely; the penalty for failing to do so is the possibility of the property being compulsorily purchased by the council. In these cases – and they are comparatively rare – the council would normally work in conjunction with a buildings preservation trust which would acquire the building from the council, repairing it for sale on the open market.

One of the surprises for owners of listed buildings is how few grants towards the repair of the building are available. People seem to imagine that either the local council or the Government has funds to assist them in any normal repairs they may wish to carry out. This is rarely the case, and any potential owner of a listed building would be most unwise to anticipate any financial assistance at all. In certain cases, English Heritage (see below) may make a grant for the repair of an outstanding listed building, or one which is in such a poor state of repair as to be seriously at risk. Some local councils have very restricted grant schemes, although there are fewer of these than once used to be the case, due to financial constraints.

The Government, in a misplaced effort to help, made a curious tax concession to owners of listed buildings some time ago. Works that alter or improve the building (where it is a dwelling or owned by a charity) are normally free from VAT, provided that they are approved. In other words, listed building consent has first to be obtained. Repairs, which one would think the Government would seek to encourage, are not subject to this concession, which is the surprising outcome of what seems to be a bureaucratic misunderstanding at the highest level. Many years of campaigning by conservation societies and other organizations for a change to this situation, and for the lifting of VAT from repair costs, have come to nought.

Conservation Areas

It is often imagined that conservation areas are as powerful in protecting groups of historic buildings as the listed building laws. This is not the case, although some improvements were brought about in 1995, partly as a result of the *Townscape in Trouble* campaign run by the English Historic Towns Forum, and pressure from the National Amenity Societies (see below). A new streamlined provision allows local authorities to remove 'permitted development rights' (see below under planning permission) from certain categories of buildings, resulting in considerable control over changes that might affect the appearance of the conservation area.

The 'conservation area' was the invention of Lord Duncan Sandys who, with the support of the Civic Trust (see below) brought the Civic Amenities Act (1967) through Parliament as a private member's bill. The idea was to protect the best areas of towns and villages, considering not only the buildings themselves, but also the spaces between, such as town squares and village greens. It required councils to consider the special character and appearance of the conservation area when deciding planning applications, and provided protection from demolition for all of the buildings and many other structures (such as boundary walls) in the area. In a later amendment it also provided protection for trees, although this was not extended to control new tree planting, even where this may destroy beautiful views.

As the result of owners of buildings in conservation areas having fewer permitted development rights, many smaller-scale alterations, and all cases involving the demolition of a building, require applications for permission to the local council. Usually this takes the form of an ordinary application for planning permission, but where any significant demolition is involved, also requires an application for 'conservation area consent'.

Planning Permission

For any significant alterations or extensions to a building, or for changes of use of buildings or land, and of course for new development, planning permission will be required. What does and does not require permission is detailed in the current General Development Order, a very complicated document that each Planning Officer at a local council will usually have to hand. Work that the Order says does not require planning permission is known as 'permitted development'.

The key background document to the planning system is the development plan. In the Cotswolds (as in most rural areas) this is split into two separate plans: the County Structure Plan, which deals with strategic matters, and the Local Plan, which has detailed policies. Planning permission will normally be granted for proposals in line with the development plan unless 'material considerations' indicate that another decision would be more appropriate. Ugly designs, for example, are more likely to be refused if they affect a listed building, or impinge on a conservation area, than if they are proposed elsewhere. The effect of a proposal on the neighbourhood is a very important factor, and one that often results in intense local debate.

The effect of increased traffic, noise or pollution are also significant considerations, while the prevention of development sprawl into the countryside has always been one of the most crucial aspects of the planning law. To emphasise this point the principal Act is called 'The Town and Country Planning Act'.

Building Regulations

The actual technical means of the construction of a building is generally subject to the Building Regulations. First created to deal with the poor construction, ventilation, and drainage of Victorian slums, these regulations now control such things as the thermal insulation of external walls, and form part of the Government's energy-saving campaign. Also, recently, there has been increased recognition of the need to provide for disabled people, and this now forms another part of the Regulations. They also deal with the important issue of means of escape from the building in the event of a fire.

There can be difficulties where historic buildings are involved. Old methods of construction are often not as required by the Regulations, and can only be rendered acceptable by major and often insensitive changes to the historic details of the building. In such cases, the Government has asked local councils to allow for a relaxation of the tight requirements, especially where the building is listed.

Environmental Health Restrictions

While the Building Regulations deal with most aspects of building construction, the local council's Environmental Health Officer may also be involved in considering whether the building is fit to be used as a dwelling. Concerns include the size of rooms and the amount of natural lighting. The lack of modern kitchens or bathrooms and toilets can also be a problem, and, in conjunction with other defects, could ultimately result in the service of a 'Closing Order' under the Housing Act (1980). If the building is not listed (see above) the local council can, in extreme cases, seek the demolition of the building.

Many decaying historic buildings – long since abandoned but now available for sale to keen conservation-oriented owners – may be subject to closing orders, and it is always worth checking this with the relevant Environmental Health Officer. They would have to agree to have any such order lifted, and will therefore advise on what work has to be carried out. The provisions of the Housing Act are also particularly important where a building has been converted to flats.

USEFUL ADDRESSES

English Heritage and Government Conservation Agencies

English Heritage, South-West Region, Room 309, 23 Savile Row, London, W1X 1AB. Telephone: 0171-973 3000.

English Heritage (whose full name is the 'Historic Buildings and Monuments Commission for England) was created by the Government in 1984 to take over all of the building conservation duties formerly carried out by the Department of the Environment. The Cotswolds lie mostly within their South-West Region, although Oxfordshire is in the South-East Area (based in Room 302) and Warwickshire is in the West-Midlands Area (based in Room 323).

The area teams tend to deal with proposals affecting the higher grades of listed buildings (see above), but can also be a useful source of specialist advice. If grant aid from English Heritage is being discussed, this should be through the area team. Initially, however, contact should be made with the Conservation Officer of the local council.

Department of Culture, Media and Sport, 2-4 Cockspur Street, London, SW1Y 5DH. Telephone: 0171-211 6000

After the creation of English Heritage, some legal functions continued to be administered by the Department of the Environment. In 1992 the Government created a new department which would deal with such matters as the listing of buildings, approval for compulsory purchase of listed buildings, and a few other legal matters. (It was given its present, rather lengthy, new name after the change of Government in 1997.) However, planning matters, such as dealing with appeals against refusal of permission, are still dealt with by the Department of the Environment, Transport and the Regions, occasionally resulting in some confusion between the two Government departments.

Royal Commission on the Historical Monuments of England, National Monuments Record Centre, Kemble Drive, Swindon, Wilts. SN2 2GZ. Telephone: 01793 414764.

This standing Royal Commission was created in 1908 to provide a record of archaeology and buildings in England. The Commission has one of the largest collections of photographs of building in the country, all housed in parish-by-parish box files held in the new National Record Centre in Swindon. These are available for public inspection.

There is a further statutory role for the Commission in that applications affecting the historic structure of listed buildings must be notified to the Commission, so that they can decide whether the building merits recording, either by photographs, a report, or a drawn record. If this is not done, permissions become invalid.

Heritage Lottery Fund, 7 Holbein Place, London, SW1W 8NR. Telephone: 0171-591 6000.

Created in 1993 and administered under the auspices of the National Heritage Memorial Fund (NHMF) the Heritage Lottery Fund (HLF) is the distributing body for the very significant National Lottery money intended for 'the Heritage'. While English Heritage grant aid is now much more restricted to assisting only 'outstanding' buildings, the HLF has taken over as the major source of grant aid for building conservation projects in the public sector or where they are owned by charities or the voluntary sector. Recent new powers will enable the HLF to assist private property, although this is likely to be through comprehensive schemes of regeneration or more urban conservation rather than through individual one-off projects.

National Amenity Societies

These are the six conservation societies, originally set up with a range of objectives, now all given official status by being built into the legislation governing listed buildings. Local councils have to consult these societies when they receive applications involving the demolition or partial demolition of listed buildings. Five of the societies are open to membership by the general public, and all are worth joining by those with the relevant architectural interests.

The Society for the Protection of Ancient Buildings (SPAB), 37 Spital Square, London, E1 6DY. Telephone: 0171-377 1644.

This was the first of the National Amenity Societies, founded by William Morris in 1877. It now concentrates on cases relating to pre-1700 buildings, and produces a comprehensive set of technical pamphlets and information sheets on the repair of historic buildings, several being of particular relevance to Cotswold architecture and lime technology (see Chapter 2).

The Ancient Monuments Society, St Ann's Vestry Hall, 2 Church Entry, London, EC4V 5HB. Telephone: 0171-236 3934.

Founded in 1934 in Manchester, this organization places great emphasis on the study of historic buildings, and to support this it publishes a well-respected annual *Transactions*. It works closely with the Friends of Friendless Churches, campaigning for the preservation of churches otherwise due for demolition. One special role adopted by the Society is the compilation of an annual register of cases where listed buildings are proposed for demolition, reporting on progress with each case in the regular newsletters.

The Georgian Group, 6 Fitzroy Square, London, W1P 6DX. Telephone: 0171-387 1720.

The Group was founded in 1937 to provide a special voice for the preservation of eighteenth- and early nineteenth-century buildings. It has led to an increased understanding and appreciation of Georgian and Regency architecture and, like the other societies, has published practical guides for owners. Beside application casework, its principal activity is in organizing visits to Georgian buildings and sites.

The Victorian Society, 1 Priory Gardens, Bedford Park, London, W4 1TT. Telephone: 0181-994 1019.

Like the Georgian Group, the Victorian Society was formed in 1958 in response to the apparent lack of public appreciation of Victorian architecture. Visits to Victorian places are arranged, and it too has just started to produce guides for owners of Victorian buildings. Part of its specialist role is commenting on applications affecting listed buildings of the Victorian period.

The Twentieth Century Society, 70 Cowcross, London, EC1M 6BP. Telephone: 0171-250 3857.

It seems as if the amenity societies are overtaking history, especially with this newest organization, formerly called 'The Thirties Society'. Founded in 1979 originally to support the preservation of interwar architecture, its brief has recently expanded to deal with all post-1914 architecture.

The Council for British Archaeology, Bowes Morrell House, 111 Walmgate, York, YO1 2UA. Telephone: 01904 671417.

Principally set up as a co-ordinating body for the various local and regional archaeological societies, it now carries out casework on the more significant applications affecting listed buildings. The membership of this society is mainly institutional.

Other National Building Conservation or Research Organizations

Association for Studies in the Conservation of Historic Buildings (ASCHB), Stephen Marks (*Transaction* Editor), Hamilton's, Kilmersdon, Bath, Somerset.

Membership is intended for those working professionally in the field of building conservation, and is by invitation. However, the invaluable *Transactions* are available for sale to the public, and contain articles ranging from the highly technical, to those of more general interest.

The Civic Trust, 17 Carlton House Terrace, London, SW1Y 5AW. Telephone: 0171-930 0914.

A society formed especially to promote the improvement of towns and cities, and also the body to which many local civic societies are affiliated. It is a useful source of information on the civic societies operating in the area, and worth contacting to find the address of the local society.

Council for the Protection of Rural England (CPRE), Warwick House, 25 Buckingham Palace Road, London, SW1W 0PP. Telephone: 0171-976 6433.

A very active campaign organization, also very much based on local branches and sub-branches. Generally less involved with buildings in detail, although does take the longer view, concerning itself with changes to the countryside. This address provides the first point of contact to find the address of the local sub-branch.

English Historic Towns Forum (EHTF), PO Box 22, Bristol, BS16 1RZ. Telephone: 0117 975-0459.

An organization having the intention to promote prosperity and conservation in the many significant historic towns and cities which are the responsibility of its local authority members. With an ambitious publishing programme, the Forum seeks to inform widely about various approaches to conservation, and influence Government where necessary, such as the largely successful *Townscape in Trouble* campaign.

SAVE Britain's Heritage, 68 Battersea High Street, London, SW11 3HX. Telephone: 0181-228 3336.

This conservation pressure group tends to get involved in campaigns to oppose demolition or neglect of some of the more important historic buildings, but also publishes a very useful report on 'Buildings at Risk', mostly compiled from information sent in by local councils. The latest edition of this report is usually a good starting point for those seeking a particularly derelict building to restore, although in the Cotswolds there are thankfully very few of these.

Vernacular Architecture Group (VAG), Mr R A Meeson, Secretary, 16 Falna Crescent, Coton Green, Tamworth, Staffs. B79 8JS. Telephone: 01827 69434.

Founded to study regional traditional buildings, the VAG now produces an annual journal, *Vernacular Architecture* and organizes twice-yearly conferences.

Local Authorities

These are the district councils that deal with planning, conservation and building matters on a day-to-day basis. Normally, if proposals do not go as far as extensions, and especially if the building is listed or in a conservation area, the person to contact is the Conservation Officer. Where more extensive works are proposed, a Planning Officer may also be involved, while building construction matters are dealt with by Building Control Officers. (The titles of council staff, known as 'officers', may vary from place to place.)

Cotswold District Council, Trinity Road, Cirencester, Glos. GL7 1PX. Telephone: 01285 643643.

North Wiltshire District Council, Monkton Park, Chippenham, Wilts. SN15 1JN. Telephone: 01249 443322.

Stratford District Council, Elizabeth House, Church Street, Stratford-upon-Avon, Warwickshire, CV37 6HY. Telephone: 01789 267575.

Stroud District Council, Ebley Mill, Stroud, Glos. GL5 4UB. Telephone: 01453 766321.

Tewkesbury Borough Council, Council Offices, Gloucester Road, Tewkesbury, Glos. GL20 5TT. Telephone: 01684 295010.

West Oxfordshire District Council, Wood Green, Witney, Oxford, OX8 6NB. Telephone: 01993 702941.

Wychavon District Council, 37 High Street, Pershore, Worcs. WR10 1AH. Telephone: 01386 565000.

Professional Organizations

When seeking your professional advisor, it is sensible to contact the relevant institute listed below to find who is practising in the area. The Architects and Surveyors Institute is, as its name suggests, an organization with members from both professions. However, its membership also includes architects that are not members of the RIBA and non-chartered surveyors. The most recently-formed institute is the Institute of Historic Building Conservation, principally intended for Conservation Officers in local authority employment, but with membership also available to other professionals actively involved in historic building conservation.

Royal Institute of British Architects (RIBA), 66 Portland Place, London, W1N 4AD. Telephone: 071-580-5533.

Royal Institute of Chartered Surveyors (RICS), 12 Great George Street, London, SW1P 3AD. Telephone: 071-222-7000.

Architects and Surveyors Institute, St Mary House, 15 St Mary Street, Chippenham Wilts. SN15 3JN. Telephone: 0249-444505.

Institute of Historic Building Conservation, Old Laundry Cottage, Mote Road, Ivy Hatch, Sevenoaks, Kent, TN15 0NT.

Operating Cotswold Quarries

The following is a list of stone quarries in the Cotswolds. The first list covers quarries producing dressed stonework and architectural elements, such as stone-mullioned windows. However, these may also be made by specialist masonry workshops which are not located at quarries, and it is recommended that a list of such masons is requested from the relevant local council Conservation Officer. The second part of the list shows those making stone slates for roofing.

Dressed Building Stone and Architectural Elements

ARC Southern Ltd, Guiting Quarry, Temple Guiting, Winchcombe, Cheltenham, Glos. GL54 5SB. Telephone: 01373 453333.

ARC operate the Coscombe Quarry which produces the classic rich orange 'Guiting' stone, but also a paler cream/white walling stone.

Cotswold Stone Quarries, Brockhill Quarry, Naunton, Cheltenham, Glos. GL54 3BA. Telephone: 01451 850775.

The Cotswold Hill Quarry produces a stone, creamy yellow in colour, suitable for use over much of the mid-Cotswolds.

Farmington Quarry, Northleach, Cheltenham, Glos. GL54 3NZ. Telephone: 01451 860280.

Generally this stone is somewhat paler in colour than Cotswold Hill, so is used over the mid- and south Cotswolds where local producers of the Painswick and Minchinhampton stones no longer exist.

Smith & Sons (Bletchington) Ltd, Enslow, Kidlington, Oxford, OX5 3AY. Telephone: 01869 331281.

The Fish Hill Quarry, operated by this company, is located between Chipping Campden and Broadway, and as expected, produces the richer 'iron stone' of the north Cotswolds, as seen on many buildings in those two towns. The quarry also has lighter-coloured beds which are worth investigation for use in the more southerly Cotswolds.

Stanleys Quarry, Northwick Estate, Upton Wold, Moreton-in-Marsh, Glos. GL56 9TR. Telephone: 01386 841236.

Generally very similar to Fish Hill Quarry, this quarry produces three colours of stone, the darkest having a strong orange-brown hue. It is marketed as 'Campden Stone'.

Natural Stone Roofing Slates

At the time of writing, there is only one quarry in the Cotswolds producing natural stone slates on a commercial scale. The slates produced near Naunton are of the type called 'presents', frost-split slates are not currently being made. Increasing efforts to revive the craft are likely to see two or three new quarries opening, and one near Corsham (owned by the Completely Stoned Company) should soon be in full production. The creation of a Cotswold Stone Slate Trust is encouraging further research into stone slate production, and it is hoped that slates split from 'Pendle' will soon also be available again. Slates made from stone imported from France in block are a surprisingly good match for local slates, especially as they are made into slates by local Cotswold craftsmen.

Cotswold Stone Quarries, Brockhill Quarry, Naunton, Cheltenham, Glos. GL54 3BA. Telephone: 01451 850775.

The Completely Stoned Company Ltd, Wedhampton Manor, Devizes, Wilts. SN10 3QE. Telephone: 01380 840092.

Many of the above quarries also supply rough-dressed building or walling stone in a variety of sizes and finishes. There are also several other quarries producing this type of stone, which is used on the majority of Cotswold buildings. Such quarries vary greatly in size, and therefore period of operation, so it is not possible to provide a list here. It is recommended that the Conservation Officer of the relevant area is contacted to obtain information on these quarries.

Suppliers of Lime Products

Bleaklow Industries Ltd, Hassop Avenue, Hassop, Bakewell, Derbyshire, DE45 1NS. Telephone: 01246 582284.

Produce a matured lime putty.

H J Chard & Sons, Albert Road, Bristol, BS2 0XS. Telephone: 0117-977 7681.

A good general supplier of lime-related products, such as lime putty, ready-mixed mortars, aggregates for mortars and renders, and natural pigments for washes.

Cy-Pres, 14 Bells Close, Brigstock, Kettering, Northants., NN14 3JG. Telephone: 01536 373431.

Supply a wide variety of traditional lime mortars and ready-mixed renders and limewashes.

I J P Building Conservation, Hollow Tree Cottage, Binfield Heath, Henley-on-Thames, Oxon. RG9 4LR. Telephone: 01734 462697.

Suppliers of lime putty, mortars and plasters.

Liz Induni, 11 Park Road, Swanage, Dorset, BH19 2AA.
Telephone: 01929 423776.

Suppliers of limewashes in a variety of colours, many traditional in the Cotswolds.

Rose of Jerico at St Blaise Ltd, Westhill Barn, Evershot, Dorchester, Dorset, DT2 0LD. Telephone: 01935 83676 or 01935 83662.

Suppliers of a complete range of lime mortars, plasters and washes.

Severn Valley Stone Co., 63 Church Street, Tewkesbury, Glos. GL20 5RZ.
Telephone: 01684 297102.

Supplies lime putty and ready-mixed mortars in larger quantities.

Speedlime, East Butts, Dunsford, Exeter, Devon, EX6 7DF.
Telephone: 01647 252161.

Supplier of lime putty.

The Traditional Lime Co., Church Farm, Leckhampton, Cheltenham, Glos.
GL51 5XX.
Telephone: 01242 525444.

Supplier of lime putties and ready-mixed mortars and renders.

Woodchester Mansion Trust Ltd (see address below).

Suppliers of lime putty.

Training in Stonemasonry and Lime Methods

Training is important for those who intend to carry out repairs to their own homes, especially if lime products are being used for the first time. The courses listed here vary between full-time courses aimed at masons and builders, to part-time and weekend courses, and courses for non-professionals.

City of Bath College, Avon Street, Bath, BA1 1UP. Telephone: 01225-312191.

The nearest place to run full-time masonry courses in the Cotswold area.

Weymouth College, Newstead Road, Weymouth, Dorset, DT4 0DX. Telephone: 01305 208946.

Has a good reputation for training in the conservation of masonry.

National Historical Building Craft Institute (NHBCI), Titanic Business Centre, Waterside South, Lincoln, LN5 7JL. Telephone: 01522 534750.

Runs long and short courses in masonry.

The Orton Trust, Wychwood, Holcot Road, Walgrave, Northants., NN6 9QN. Telephone: 01604 781326.

Variety of masonry courses available.

The Lime Centre, Long Barn, Morestead, Winchester, Hants, SO21 1LZ. Telephone: 01962 713636.

Short courses in lime mortars, plaster, renders and limewashes.

Rory Young, 5/7 Park Street, Cirencester, Glos. GL7 2BX. Telephone: 01285 658826.

Occasional courses in lime mortars, renders and limewashes.

Woodchester Mansion Trust, 1 The Old Town Hall, Stroud, Glos. GL5 1AP. Telephone: 01453 750455.

The Woodchester Mansion Trust was set up to repair and conserve Woodchester Mansion, the great unfinished Victorian-Gothic country house set in National Trust parkland three miles south of Stroud. Its second objective is education in the conservation of historic buildings, especially in stonemasonry. The Trust runs a range of training courses, master-classes, and weekend courses in stone repairs and lime mortars, and can offer individual 'technical briefings' on particular techniques or buildings.

BIBLIOGRAPHY

Ager, Donovan, Kennedy, McKerrow, Mudge, Sellwood, *The Cotswold Hills*, Geologists' Association Guide No. 36, The Geologists' Association, 1973.

Aldred, David H., *Cleeve Hill, The History of the Common and its People*, Alan Sutton, 1990.

Ashurst, John, *Mortars, Plasters and Renders in Conservation*, Ecclesiastical Architects' and Surveyors' Association, 1983.

Ashurst, John and Nicola, *Practical Building Conservation*, English Heritage/Gower Technical Press, 1988.

Ashurst, John and Dimes, Francis G., *Stone in Building*, The Architectural Press, 1977.

Barley, Maurice, *The English Farmhouse and Cottage*, Routledge and Kegan Paul, 1961.

Barley, Maurice, *Houses and History*, Faber and Faber, 1986.

Brill, Edith, *Life and Tradition on the Cotswolds*, Alan Sutton, 1987.

Brunskill, R.W., *Traditional Buildings of Britain*, Victor Gollancz, 1982.

Bullard, Peter (ed.), *A Revised Inventory of Gloucestershire's Ancient Woodlands: The Cotswold Plateau*, The Gloucestershire Trust for Nature Conservation, 1987.

Clifton-Taylor, Alec, *The Pattern of English Building*, Faber and Faber, 1972.

Clifton-Taylor, Alec and Ireson, A.S., *English Stone Building*, Victor Gollancz, 1983.

Coldstream, Nicola, *Masons and Sculptors*, British Museum Press, 1991.

Cook, Olive, *English Cottages and Farmhouses*, Thames and Hudson, 1982.

Cumming, Elizabeth and Kaplan, Wendy, *The Arts and Crafts Movement*, Thames and Hudson, 1991.

Darley, Gillian, *Villages of Vision*, Granada Publishing, 1978.

Davey, Peter, *Arts and Crafts Architecture: The Search for Earthly Paradise*, The Architectural Press, 1980.

Davie, W. Galsworthy and Dawber, E. Guy, *Old Cottages, Farm-Houses and other Stone Buildings in the Cotswold District*, Batsford, 1905.

Dreghorn, William, *Geology Explained in the Severn Vale and Cotswolds*, David & Charles, 1973.

Evans, H.A., with engravings by Griggs, F., *Highways and Byways in Oxford and the Cotswolds*, MacMillan and Co., 1905.

Fawcett, Jane (ed.), *The Future of the Past*, Thames and Hudson, 1976.

Feilden, Bernard M., *Conservation of Historic Buildings*, Butterworths, 1982.

Finberg, H.R.P., *The Gloucestershire Landscape*, Hodder and Stoughton, 1975.

Finberg, Josceline, *The Cotswolds*, Eyre Methuen, 1977.

Gibbs, J. Arthur, *A Cotswold Village*, John Murray, 1909.

Greensted, Mary, *Gimson and the Barnsleys*, Alan Sutton, 1992.

Greensted, Mary, *The Arts and Crafts Movement in the Cotswolds*, Alan Sutton, 1993.

Hadfield, Charles and Alice (eds.), *The Cotswolds: A New Study*, David & Charles, 1973.

Hall, Linda, *The Rural Houses of North Avon & South Gloucestershire: 1400–1720*, City of Bristol Museum & Art Gallery, Monograph No. 6, 1983.

Jewson, Norman, *By Chance I Did Rove*, Gryffon Publications, 1986.

Lambert, M.D. and Shipman, Juliet, *The Unknown Cotswold Village: Eastcombe 1500–1980*, 1981.

Lander, Hugh, *A Guide to the Do's & Don'ts of House and Cottage Conversion*, Acanthus Books, 1982.

Lander, Hugh, *A Guide to the Do's & Don'ts of House & Cottage Interiors*, Acanthus Books, 1982.

Lander, Hugh, *The House Restorer's Guide*, David & Charles, 1986.

Leech, Roger, *Historic Towns in Gloucestershire*, Committee for Rescue Archaeology in Avon, Gloucestershire and Somerset, 1981.

Lees-Milne, James, *Some Cotswold Country Houses*, The Dovecote Press, 1987.

McGlone, G., *Gloucestershire Commons, Their History, Wildlife and Future*, Gloucestershire Trust for Nature Conservation, 1989.

Mills, Stephen and Riemer, Pierce, *The Mills of Gloucestershire*, Barracuda Books, 1989.

Moriarty, Denis, *Buildings of the Cotswolds*, Victor Gollancz, 1989.

Parsons, David (ed.), *Stone: Quarrying and Building in England – AD 43–1525*, Phillimore, 1990.

Perkins, J.W., Brooks, A.T., and Pearce, A.E.McR., *Bath Stone, A Quarry History*, Department of Extra-mural Studies, University College, Cardiff, 1990.

Peters, J.E.C., *Discovering Traditional Farm Buildings*, Shire Publications, 1981.

Powell, Christopher, *Discovering Cottage Architecture*, Shire Publications, 1984.

Quiney, Anthony, *The Traditional Buildings of England*, Thames and Hudson, 1990.

Saunders, Matthew, *The Historic Home Owner's Companion*, Batsford, 1987.

Saville, Alan (ed.), *Archaeology in Gloucestershire*, Cheltenham Art Gallery and Museums and The Bristol and Gloucestershire Archaeological Society, 1984.

Shadmon, Asher, *Stone – An Introduction*, Intermediate Technology Publications, 1989.

Smith, Brian, *The Cotswolds*, Alan Sutton, 1992.

Verey, David, *Buildings of England: Gloucestershire: The Cotswolds*, Penguin, 1979.

William, Richard, *Limekilns and Limeburning*, Shire Publications, 1989.

Witts, Revd. F.E., (ed. David Verey), *The Diary of a Cotswold Parson*, Alan Sutton, 1979.

Wood, Margaret, *The English Mediaeval House*, Bracken Books, 1983.

Wood-Jones, Raymond B., *Traditional Domestic Architecture in the Banbury Region*, Wykham Books, 1986.

Wright, Adela, *Craft Techniques for Traditional Buildings*, Batsford, 1991.

Wright, Geoffrey N., *The Cotswolds*, David & Charles, 1991.

INDEX

References to illustrations are in italics and to colour pictures by C and the illustration number.